# THE DEFINITIVE COCKTAIL BO

*In the same series*

The Right Wine With The Right Food
Home Winemaking the Right Way

# THE DEFINITIVE COCKTAIL BOOK

Jeffrey Benson and Stuart Walton

RIGHT WAY

Constable & Robinson Ltd
3 The Lanchesters
162 Fulham Palace Road
London W6 9ER

www.constablerobinson.com

First published in the UK 2004
This edition published by Right Way, an imprint
of Constable & Robinson, 2010



A copy of the British Library Cataloguing in Publication Data
is available from the British Library

ISBN: 978-0-7160-2168-1
Printed and bound in the EU

# CONTENTS

# DEDICATION

Mr Benson dedicates this book to his wife Clare, and Mr Walton to his trusty and stalwart friend, Chris Tothill.

# INTRODUCTION

Every age rediscovers cocktails for itself, and every age seems to reinvent the basic idea of the drink. When a shiny, monochrome new bar opens on the high street, we scarcely bat an eyelid to see, alongside the imported beers and global wines, a bar list offering us the likes of Chocolate-Nut Martini (Plymouth gin, white crème de cacao and Frangelico) and Shamrock Espresso (Absolut vodka, Bailey's Irish Cream, butterscotch schnapps and espresso coffee). It wasn't always this way, though.

In the postwar years, cocktails had almost faded from view. Many households boasted something called a cocktail cabinet, but instead of being stocked with alcohol treasures from the four corners of the earth, they came instead to hold glasses and ice-buckets, and perhaps the odd bottle of gin or whisky for when friends came to call. The concept of the cocktail party had receded into the past, where it featured as an indispensable aspect of our idea of the roaring twenties, the age of tittering flappers, the silent movies, *The Great Gatsby* and Prohibition.

Their first great revival of recent years came in the early 1980s, when they formed an essential part of the lifestyle of a group of movers and shakers in fashion and music known as the New Romantics. Image-consciousness was everything: girls' shoulders were padded robustly enough to allow them to engage in contact sports, while the boys looked as though they had paid rather more attention to their hair than was quite healthy in red-blooded males. What everybody drank was cocktails, and cocktail bars – which had previously not been heard of outside the confines of grand hotels – sprang up in every town and city in the UK to cater for the new craze.

As New Romanticism gave way to the Hard Times look during a period of economic privation, cocktails suddenly seemed too frivolous, and it was all export-strength beer and cheap spirits again. The beginning of the 1990s saw the introduction of 'shooters', short-sharp-shock drinks served in tiny glasses that represented something of a compromise between the old type of flamboyant drink (often served in something resembling a flower-vase and replete with sparklers, parasols and tropical fruit) and the new austerity. Shooters were lethally strong mixtures, often consisting entirely of alcohol, intended to be downed in one.

In the last few years, cocktails have made a big comeback, but with another twist. The hard, fast drinking of the shooters has given way to a softer, schmoozier style of cocktail, where the mixture is often of different fruit juices on a single alcohol base. Consider the sudden popularity of the 1960s recipe Sea Breeze, which is plain vodka dressed to impress with cranberry and grapefruit juices, a pleasing mixture and potentially a strong one if drunk in the kinds of places where they pour freehand instead of measuring out, but essentially not much more than a new twist on the old vodka-and-fruit-juice formula that began with the Screwdriver.

An interesting aspect of the new cocktails is that the ingredients are very often chosen to mask the flavour of alcohol, for people who don't especially enjoy the taste of it, but do quite like its effect. This is the case where sweet, fruity liqueurs play a dominant part in a mix, as much as when fizzy mixers such as Coca-Cola and ginger ale do, and it is also why the more neutral spirits, such as vodka, white rum and silver tequila, are widely favoured over the more assertive likes of gin or whisky.

That impulse to hide the alcohol, rather than play it up, harks back unwittingly to the cocktail era of the 1920s, when, in the United States at least, the recipes were all about masking the fetid taste of bootleg spirit in an era when alcohol was officially illegal. Over in Europe, where no such restrictions applied, the twenties were a period of wild experimentation as the full range of traditional spirits was used in often violent, always stimulating, combinations with the old Victorian liqueurs, as well as those of more ancient lineage, such as the famous monastic distillates of Bénédictine and Chartreuse. The liqueurs were, in a sense, rescued from what could well have been terminal decline in the twentieth century by the original and greatest modern cocktail era. Suddenly there was a crying need for bright green crème de menthe and the honey-based Scotch liqueurs that went beyond the annual predilections of infirm relatives at Christmas.

The Jazz Age also spawned the first publishing boom in cocktail books (its presiding genius was the great Harry Craddock of the American Bar at London's Savoy Hotel, whose *Savoy Cocktail Book* remains an essential reference-point today), and we have drawn resourcefully on our treasured copies of these to bring you a few of the early versions of what are now classic formulas (as well as a few that probably haven't seen the light of day since the Wall Street Crash) in the recipes contained herein.

Reaching back still further into the late nineteenth century, we find a less extravagant tradition of mixed drinks, some of which may be fairly said to be the prototypes of what was to follow, but most of which were little more than slight modifications of basic spirits, usually involving the addition of a few drops of bitters and perhaps some sugar to balance them. Mixed drinks were given their first real lease of life in this era under the tutelage of the granddaddy of all cocktail barmen, 'Professor' Jerry Thomas of the Occidental Hotel in San Francisco, author of the first bartender's guide and inventor of many classics of the repertoire, including – some say – the original Martini.

In this sanguine bygone era, cocktails were drunk at all times of the day, but especially before dinner, not so much as appetite-honing aperitifs, but as the marker that announced the end of the afternoon and the beginning of the evening. To this day in the USA, you will quite often find yourself being invited to take a 'cocktail' with companions at six o'clock or soon after. What is being offered is not something with at least four ingredients that has to be whooshed up in a shaker, but a simple mixed drink – a whisky sour or gin and tonic, say – that fulfils the function of separating off the business part of the day from its recreational coda.

As we glance retrospectively back, one of the oldest questions in any book such as ours must be squared up to. What is the origin of the word 'cocktail'? Authors have been having a go at answering this question since the very first recipe books were published in the nineteenth century. It remains officially unknown, although theories that have been floated include the following.

1. The name refers to the habit of decorating flagons of drink with feathers from cocks' tails, a custom dating back to the Elizabethan era.

2. English buccaneers travelling in the Gulf of Mexico in the sixteenth century came upon a local custom in which mixtures of the rudimentary distilled drinks of the region were stirred up with a root that looked like a cock's tail, and was indeed known in the Spanish as a *cola de gallo*.

3. It is a corruption of the name given to a mixed drink fed to fighting cocks in the eighteenth century, known as 'cock-ale'.

(These can be safely torpedoed, we think, on the grounds that the term would have been in use since the relevant period each tale respectively refers to, whereas the earliest recorded usage of the word only appears in the first decade of the nineteenth century.)

4. It arose at American race meetings in the early 1800s as a drink with which one toasted the chances of racehorses with tails like those of cockerels, or that were cocked up (i.e. stuck up in the air). There is indeed a distinguished subset of cocktails associated with Derby Days and horse races generally in the Southern States, the most pre-eminent of which is the whisky-based Mint Julep, but nothing prevents this theory from being tenuous in the extreme. Why would all mixed drinks come to be known as cocktails? Why, even, would one name the drink after the fashion of the horse's tail specifically, as opposed to the more general milieu of the horse race?

5. It has some connection with the recipe for a Bordeaux-based French wine cup called *coquetel*, imported by French officers serving with George Washington's army during America's revolutionary period.

6. The name dates from an incident on a Mississippi river steamer some time in the nineteenth century when a bored passenger asked for a drink to be mixed up for him that contained a little of everything available in the bar. It was served in a large, bulbous glass that looked like the breast of a cockerel, so that when the stirrers were added to it they resembled the bird's tail feathers, and the drink was named a 'cocktail'.

There are many more – mostly considerably more far-fetched than those summarised here. One of your two authors, Mr Walton, has long inclined to another view, which he here offers for your own idle perusal.

The word appears to arise at almost the precise moment – somewhere between 1806 and 1809, that is – at which it also came into use to denote one of those cock-tailed horses at the American racecourses. These were animals that, although held to be of racing quality, were not the thoroughbred article. By mid-century, this usage had undergone a metaphorical shift so that it also could be used to refer disparagingly to people. William Makepeace Thackeray, in a now little-known novel called *The Newcomes* (1855), has one of the characters roundly dismissed as 'such a . . . coxcomb as that, such a cocktail'. It now referred to somebody showy, ostentatious, foppish, somebody good at masking their true origins in smart society. A cocktail is just such a drink. It is a hybrid, rather than the unblended thoroughbred creature, showy in presentation, and given to cleverly disguising its true nature – the spirituous liquor on which it is based – beneath an outer coat of bitters, sugar, water, mint, even eggs or cream.

However that may be decided (and it probably never will be), cocktails continue to endure. It is the sheer variety made possible by the potentially limitless combinations of drinks, alcoholic and non-alcoholic, that keeps us returning to them, even when we tell ourselves we perhaps ought to have grown out of them by now. While demanding the utmost respect for their potency, they lure us into an area where drinking is indubitably fun once again, releasing us from the habitual treadmill of G&Ts, draught beer and Chardonnay. They restore creativity and adventurousness to the serious business of drinking, and our book is intended as a celebration of that fact.

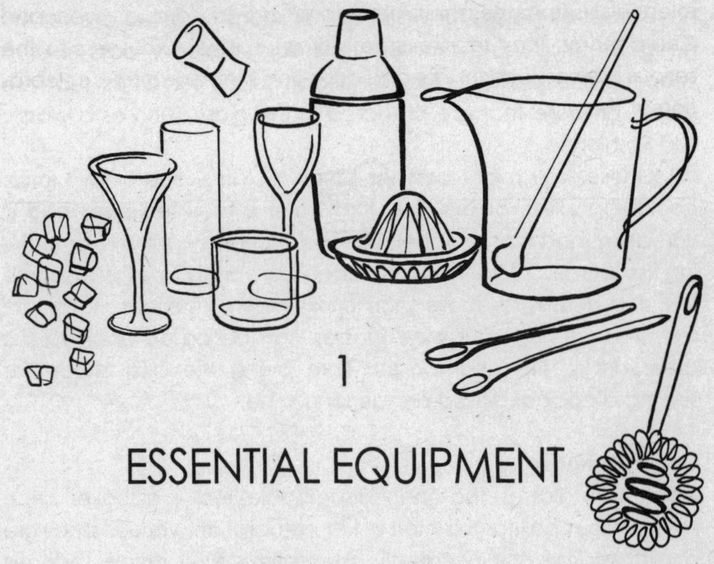

# 1

# ESSENTIAL EQUIPMENT

Before embarking on home cocktail-making, it is as well to be aware that there is rather more paraphernalia involved in the pastime than there is in any other branch of drinking. To be able to make a comprehensive range of cocktails, and look at all professional while you are about it, will mean adding significantly to your kitchen apparatus, or at least clearing a space in that cocktail cabinet, if you have one. The good news for beginners is that much of it can be improvised.

**Glasses**

Three basic types of cocktail glass should see you through most of the recipes in this book, although there are numerous designs on the market.

The first is the martini glass (otherwise known, and referred to herein, as the cocktail glass). Its bowl is an inverted cone sitting on a slender stem. These glasses hold a relatively modest amount, and are used widely for short, strong drinks intended to pack a punch. Secondly, a tall, narrow glass known as a Collins or highball glass for serving long drinks is essential, but you may well already have a set of glasses for water or fruit squash that will answer this need. The third useful type is the whisky tumbler or rocks glass, a wide-mouthed, squat glass used particularly for drinks that are stirred, or those that are prepared in the glass, such as a classic Old-Fashioned.

To these, you might add, as fancy dictates, one or two large cocktail goblets, of the kind that have a rounded bowl and a flared rim (and that are often used for blended cocktails, containing fruit purées, of the tropical beach-bar variety), as well as some tiny shot-glasses for those short drinks known as shooters. For the rest, you will find your wine glasses can be called upon to suit other drinks, the champagne flute being the best shape for serving a cocktail based on sparkling wine.

**Cocktail shaker**

Apart from glasses, the one indispensable item is a shaker, since most recipes call for this method of preparation. Various styles are available, from the needlessly ostentatious silver article to those fashioned of strengthened glass. The latter type allows you to see the mixture within attractively changing colour as it is prepared, but reckless shaking with slippery hands can result in disaster, as one of us once found to both his cost and that of the carpet where it shattered. Mr Walton's mother had, as part of her wedding trousseau, a Tupperware cocktail shaker, which may now be worth millions, but wasn't much cop, as the lid on it didn't fit tightly enough. Stainless steel is by far the most durable material, and we recommend that as the best model.

You will notice that the staff in speciality cocktail bars don't use the home style of shaker, but tend to improvise with a metal container clamped over a pint glass. This is because, where there is a press of eager business at the bar, it would simply take an unfeasibly long time to keep rinsing the same few cocktail shakers over and over between drinks, whereas a bar is always plentifully supplied with glasses. For shaking at home, go for the classic design, which consists of a deep cup, over which fits a perforated cap for straining out the ice when the drink is poured, with another smaller cap to fit over that. In some models, the top cap actually screws on to the piece beneath it, but with most it just sits on top, meaning that you have to be assiduous in holding it firmly on as the drink is shaken.

If you haven't got a shaker, but are still keen to get started, any receptacle that is big enough to take the ice and drinks and has a tight-fitting lid will do. A washed-out jam jar might do in a pinch, but only if you're not expecting chic company.

**Cocktail measure**

If possible, choose a shaker that comes with its own measure. Some form of measure is essential, as the ingredients in a successful cocktail must always be in exactly the correct proportions to each other. The standard article looks like two differently sized metal cups fixed together end to end, with one half holding twice the quantity of the other (typically, 50ml and 25ml). Where there isn't a precise indicator of capacity, you can assume, for the purposes of most recipes, that the smaller side contains a measure, and the larger a double measure. In any case, a measure should be about 25ml, the same amount in which measures of spirit are served in British pubs. In the United States, they call this piece of equipment a 'jigger', a coinage that may have derived from a similarly named item of nautical apparatus.

There are obviously other ways of measuring liquids. An eggcup was the first recourse of one of us in tender youth, and is actually quite a good guide. You will probably be able to muster a large measuring-jug from the kitchen cupboard, but the problem with that is that the calibration is quite likely to start at a much higher level than the relatively small quantities needed for cocktails. It is also possible to use spoons, if one works on the principle that a tablespoon is 15ml, a dessertspoon 10ml and a teaspoon 5ml. A single measure would therefore be a tablespoon and a dessertspoon, or five teaspoons. Quite apart from looking pathetically amateurish, though, life really is too short for the spoon route. Buy a proper measure.

**Mixing jug**

For those cocktails that are stirred, not shaken, a glass pitcher (known in the States as a bar glass) is to be used. Some are tall and slender and have the appearance of an old-fashioned claret jug, while others more nearly resemble something to put cut flowers in, being wider at the bottom than at the top. They should have at least one handle (perhaps even one on each side), and be capacious enough to make several drinks at once.

Any jug, glass or otherwise, can naturally be pressed into service for this purpose. If you aren't using it to measure quantities, that kitchen measuring-jug referred to above will happily suffice.

**Bar spoon**

A long-handled spoon for stirring those mixed cocktails, or for giving a final stir to a drink served long in a tall glass, is a useful piece of specialist equipment to have. Even a tablespoon tends to be a little short for the purpose, and anyway the bowl of the spoon is too large. A true bar spoon combines length with a surprisingly delicate bowl, but if you're pushed, an ordinary spoon will have to do.

**Strainer**

A cocktail shaker, as we have seen, comes with its own built-in strainer for removing the ice from a drink as it is poured out, but stirred cocktails made in a jug will need a separate piece of equipment if the ice is not to be left in (which, however, it expressly is in some recipes). The type that you will see in use in a cocktail bar is called a Hawthorn strainer, and is comprised of a flat, pierced disc that fits over the top of a glass, with a roll of coiled metal around its circumference to help keep the ice and any other non-liquid ingredients, such as lumps of citrus peel, from being poured into the drink.

A tea-strainer is about the next best thing, but is basically too small to catch more than a single cube of ice. A kitchen sieve, on the other hand, is too large, which risks some of the painstakingly prepared cocktail missing the glass altogether. It is probably better, though a trifle messy, to hold something such as a broad-bladed knife over the rim of the mixing-jug as you pour, to keep the ice back.

**Muddler**

This piece of equipment is for crushing leaves such as mint, or grinding granulated sugar, for drinks prepared in a mixing jug (see the recipes for Mint Julep on page 64, and Brandy Smash on page 43). It is a long-handled stick with a bulb-shaped end, designed for applying downward pressure and used much like a pestle in a mortar. There is no alternative to this, as it isn't really possible to exert vertical pressure in a jug with a spoon, so if you haven't got one, best avoid those (comparatively few) recipes for which it is needed.

**Ice**

Antarctic quantities of ice are needed for a thorough-going cocktail evening, as the same ice must never be used in more than one drink. How many ice-trays do you possess, though? Better than ice-trays in this context are those clear plastic compartmented bags that are filled up with water and frozen. When the ice is needed, you squeeze each piece through the plastic into the jug or shaker. They can be slightly harder work than you're expecting, especially if you're pressing out quite a few pieces for one batch of cocktails, but they will increase your ice stocks no end.

If you're really desperate, buy large ready-made bags of ice from the supermarket freezer section. They cost around £1.50 in UK prices, which isn't particularly cost-effective when you think you could just be using your own tap water, but are good in an emergency. (In our limited experience of them, we have tended to find that the ice often comes in unmanageably big shards, which must be smashed against a hard surface to break them down.)

**Ice-shaver**

For drinks that are to be served *frappé,* or poured over a fine snow of slivered ice crystals, an ice-shaver (also known as a smasher or crusher) is the best route. You put the ice-cubes into the upper half of it, and then clamp the top down on them, while turning a handle on the side. This activates a rotary disc set with blades, which reduces them to the requisite consistency. As they naturally melt much faster than larger pieces, they should only be made immediately before they are required.

The alternative to a shaver is manual labour. Wrap the ice-cubes in a clean tea-towel or glass cloth and pound them viciously with a wooden mallet (the kind used for tenderising beef is best). The end of a rolling-pin makes a rather clumsier way of doing the job. It hardly bears stating that bashing up ice in this way will get very tedious indeed when there are several rounds of cocktails to be made, and in any case creates one unholy row, which may cause widespread unease and contribute to a feeling among your guests that they are putting you to unconscionable amounts of trouble.

**Citrus squeezer**

Freshly squeezed juices of lemon, orange, lime, grapefruit and their more exotic cousins are very widely used in the cocktail repertoire. There has been something of a competition in recent years among manufacturers of kitchen equipment to see who can design the most ingenious-looking contraption for this purpose. The classic one is hard to beat. The fruit is halved and then twisted down on a ridged hump, the juice pouring through holes into a dish below, from which it is then strained out.

The terminally lazy might like to resort to an electric model, but they aren't always that reliable, and continually washing them up somehow seems a lot more of a chore than it is with the manual variety.

**Electric blender/liquidiser**

This is the one piece of electrical equipment that really is indispensable for certain types of cocktail (i.e. those that contain semi-solid materials such as chopped fruit or ice-cream, or where a certain frothiness from the incorporation of egg-white is required). The tall goblet design is the best, but beware of putting whole ice-cubes into it regularly as it will gradually ruin the little blades.

For frothing egg-white, an ordinary hand-whisk will do the job, but then you will have to froth it separately to the liquid ingredients, which isn't quite the point.

**Garnishing items**

How decorative you want your drinks to look depends on individual taste, but recent fashion is to keep it plain and simple. That said, plastic straws are an option, and considered a textbook way of drinking certain cocktails. Cocktail sticks can be used for threading pieces of fruity garnish, such as cherries and citrus slices, and swizzle-sticks are handy for allowing the drinker to refresh a long cocktail that they are taking an inordinate time to drink.

Finally, a couple of things to bear in mind. Some of the recipes in this book contain raw egg yolk. Only free-range eggs should be used, but in any case, these recipes are not advisable for those with impaired immune systems, the elderly, or pregnant women.

Others call for a sprinkling of nutmeg on the surface. This should be particularly avoided by migraine sufferers.

As stated previously, one measure is 25ml/1 fl oz/5 teaspoons.

A dash is the small dribble that escapes from a bottle when it is very quickly tilted over the shaker or jug. The whole operation should take less than a second.

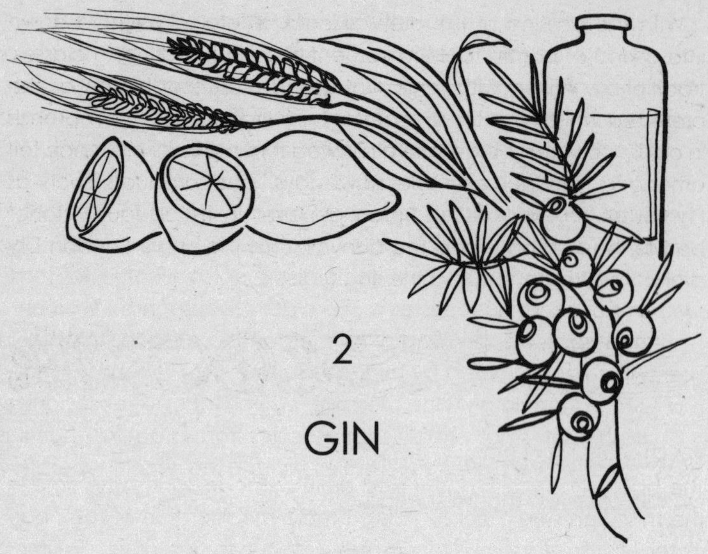

# 2

# GIN

Although its place has been usurped in many of the most fashionable cocktail recipes today by the less aromatic likes of neutral vodka and white rum, gin remains in many ways the pre-eminent base ingredient. One of the big-selling brands of gin boasted on its label for many years that it was 'The heart of a good cocktail', a statement that still holds true of the drink in general. Its peculiar, apothecarial scent, derived predominantly from juniper berries but supported by a herbalist's cabinet of aromatising plants and spices, blends improbably well with a broad range of liqueurs and non-alcoholic mixers.

The precursor product is genever, a juniper-scented grain distillate first formulated in Holland in the seventeenth century, but juniper was probably already being added to a distilled spirit in Italy as much as 500 years before that, when the art of distillation was still in its infancy in Europe. Soldiers returning from the Thirty Years' War brought the taste for Dutch gin to England, and by the following century it was being so widely produced at such low prices, both officially and illicitly, that an epidemic of gin drinking took hold of London, with catastrophic effects on public health.

With the passing of the pre-war cocktail era, gin settled down into a kind of comfortable retirement among the drinking classes, traditionally mixed with tonic water and a slice of lemon as the preferred whistle-wetter of a certain generation. Sexy new brands in oddly coloured bottles have allowed it to make its presence felt among a younger clientele nowadays, and products such as Plymouth gin, as well as Dutch genever in its opaque 'stone' bottles, have broadened the canvas from the single London Dry archetype that once had the ring to itself.

## EARLY GIN SLING

The basic structure of the mixed drink came to light some time in the mid-eighteenth century as a simple modification of the character of a spirit such as gin, usually with sugar and water. In time, lemon, where it was available, came to be added to it, its bracing sourness altering the flavour and being balanced out by the sugar. This was the basic sling.

**2 measures gin**
**1 tsp sugar, caster for preference**
**juice of half a lemon**

Mix these ingredients well with ice in a tall glass or tumbler until the sugar is quite invisible, and top up the drink with chilled still water. Add a slice of lemon if desired.

## CLASSIC GIN SLING

When the first dictionary definitions of the cocktail were written, it was initially described as 'a bittered sling'. In other words, to the sweet and sour elements already in the sling was now added a bittering component, classically in the form of the nineteenth-century South American medicinal compound, Angostura bitters, named after a town in Venezuela, and based on an infusion of gentian root and herbs. To the mixture above, add a dash or two of Angostura, before topping up with water.

## GIN SOUR

A stronger drink for the brave of heart could obviously be made by omitting the water top-up altogether, in which case the lemon juice would make its acerbic presence felt all the more, which is why this formula, thought to date from around the 1850s, was called the Gin Sour. Proportions and method should otherwise be exactly the same as for the Early Gin Sling.

## GIN FIZZ

The cocktail repertoire was given an effervescent boost in the mid-nineteenth century by the earliest use of sparkling water. The soda siphon, without which the genteel home of the period on either side of the Atlantic was scarcely complete, made fizzy drinks possible by charging plain tap water with tablets of sodium bicarbonate. Eventually, bottled soda water became economical enough to use and the soda siphon went the way of the wind-up gramophone. Some high-rollers resorted to bottles of naturally sparkling Alpine mineral water, but the risk with this is that it added an unwanted mineral flavour or saltiness to the drink. Follow the Early Gin Sling recipe again, but top with soda instead of still water. By the turn of the twentieth century, the base ingredients for the Fizz (the gin, sugar and lemon) were being routinely shaken with the ice, and then strained into the serving glass, before the soda was added.

## TOM COLLINS

There is precious little difference between the Gin Fizz and the Tom Collins, excepting that the Collins is always served in a tall, narrow glass (sometimes known as a Collins glass), and may be garnished a touch more extravagantly with a cocktail cherry and a half-slice of orange as well as lemon. It was originally known as the John Collins, but changed its name when it began to be made in the 1850s with a now-defunct brand of gin called Old Tom, which was sweeter than the succeeding norm.

## PINK GIN

As we have introduced Angostura bitters, we may as well use it for this deeply class-bound old naval recipe. Whereas the mere ratings in the Royal Navy had to make do with a ration of dark rum, the tipple of the officer class was gin, and this is how it was taken. The gin used should always be Plymouth rather than London, in acknowledgement of the importance the Devon sea-port has always played in British naval history.

Take a small goblet-style wine glass, and sprinkle six or seven droplets of Angostura bitters into it. Roll them around to moisten the inside of the glass, and then shake them out (shipboard, you would simply dash the Angostura out on the floor). Add a goodly measure or three of stone-cold Plymouth gin. The residue of the bitters should leave a very light tinge of pink (or puce, to be precise) in the drink.

## MARTINI

The origins of what is arguably the most famous cocktail of them all are as much disputed as the basic formula has been modified over the years. What is not in doubt is that its provenance lies in a simple two-way mixture of gin and a bitter-sweet additive. The recipe is American, and is generally credited now to the great San Francisco pioneer, Jerry Thomas, who is said to have created it for a guest who was passing through the hotel where he worked en route to Martinez in California. Prior to the widespread commercialisation of vermouth in the USA in the latter half of the nineteenth century, the favoured second ingredient was orange curaçao. The sweet red version of vermouth (typically thought of as the Italian style by cocktail makers) was the first to arrive, quickly supplanting curaçao in the mix, and when it was followed in the 1890s by the dry (classically French) style, the already popular Martini cocktail was joined by the more sophisticated Dry Martini. It was, theoretically, the popularity of the Martini & Rossi brand of vermouth from Turin that amended the cocktail's name from Martinez.

The Martini really should be shaken, although many like it stirred, with plenty of ice, and the drink strained into the archetypal cocktail glass that bears its name. It is the proportions that cause such dissension, with some arguing in favour of a two-to-one ratio of gin to dry vermouth, as was once traditional. Cocktail books of the 1920s often suggest a dash of orange or Angostura bitters to complete the mixture. In the ascendancy, though, is the technique of adding the dry vermouth as though it were a thousand guineas an ounce – a single dash, a single drop even. Some suggest lightly rinsing the glass with vermouth that is then discarded, like the Angostura for a Pink Gin, with the gin being shaken in splendid isolation in the ice, although the formula recommended by the International Bartenders' Association is four parts gin to one part dry vermouth, stirred, and with either a bit of lemon zest or an olive thrown in.

Apocryphal tales abound of customers who would only allow the shadow of the unopened vermouth bottle to pass across the glass, or who merely required the bartender to bow once in the direction of France before the cold gin was poured, while a lady advanced in both years and gin intake once told one of the authors in a hotel bar that her preference was for the barman simply to whisper the word 'vermouth' at the drink. While these last have, unbeknown to themselves, obviously discovered a taste for neat gin on the way to the funny farm, the sparing approach is undoubtedly the best. Something like one-eighth of a measure of dry vermouth to three measures of gin is a good guide. Squeeze a piece of lemon peel over the drink, so that the expressed oil is scattered in little globs over the surface. Add a stuffed green olive if you dare (some hate this garnish, and will refuse the resulting concoction as firmly as 'twere bitter aloes).

## SINGAPORE SLING (THE REAL THING)

Created by Ngiam Tong Boon, head bartender of the Long Bar at the legendary Raffles Hotel in Singapore during the Great War years, this much-loved cocktail isn't really any sort of sling as it wasn't originally topped up with water. It has become popular since as a long, sparkling drink filled with soda, in which case Singapore Fizz might be a more appropriate moniker. The recipe changes a little according to whoever happens to be running the bar, but this was the formula vouchsafed in person to Mr Benson during the course of exhaustive researches in the Long Bar. The quantities are given in millilitres.

**30ml gin**
**15ml cherry brandy**
**dash triple sec (Cointreau)**
**dash Bénédictine**
**60ml fresh lime juice**
**120ml pineapple juice**
**dash Angostura bitters**
**dash grenadine**

Shake all the ingredients well with ice, and strain into a highball (tall) glass. Garnish with a half-slice of orange and a cherry.

## SINGAPORE SLING (THE SHORTCUT)

**1 measure gin**

**1 measure cherry brandy**

**1 measure lemon juice**

**dash Cointreau**

**soda to top up**

Shake the first four ingredients well with ice, strain into a highball glass, and top with ice-cold soda water. Garnish as above. This version, by which no disrespect is intended to the memory of Mr Ngiam, is an accepted modern variant on the recipe.

## WHITE LADY

**1½ measures gin**

**¾ measure Cointreau**

**¾ measure lemon juice**

Shake the ingredients well with ice, and strain into a cocktail glass. A classic of the 1920s, this found its way into print in Harry Craddock's *Savoy Cocktail Book* of 1930. There has been a fashion in recent years to make it slightly frothy by adding a teaspoon of egg white, a tendency that should be mercilessly suppressed as it spoils a simple and perfect formula.

The next few recipes are for cocktails that were popular on either or both sides of the Atlantic in the 1920s. That, of course, was the era of alcohol Prohibition in the United States and some of these concoctions were as much about muffling the appalling taste of bathtub gin as they were about creating new and exciting drinks. A couple of them contain absinthe, which had been banned in much of Europe by this time, but is now thankfully restored to us once more.

## DIXIE

**1½ measures gin**

**¾ measure dry vermouth**

**¾ measure absinthe**

Shake with ice and strain into a cocktail glass. Garnish with a twist of lemon. This is a very dry and very powerful drink.

## PRINCETON

**2 measures gin**

**1 measure ruby port**

**dash orange bitters**

Stir in a mixing jug with ice until the temperature is cold enough to mist up the glass, and then strain into a cocktail glass. Squeeze a piece of lemon peel over the top.

## ULANDA

**2 measures gin**

**1 measure Cointreau**

**dash absinthe**

Shake with ice and strain into a cocktail glass. A strong cocktail to be approached with caution.

## COLONIAL

**2 measures gin**

**1 measure grapefruit juice**

**dash maraschino**

Shake with ice and strain into a cocktail glass. This is a bracingly sour cocktail that would make a good aperitif.

## JOURNALIST

**2 measures gin**

**½ measure dry vermouth**

**½ measure sweet red vermouth**

**2 dashes orange curaçao**

**2 dashes lemon juice**

**1 dash Angostura bitters**

Shake well with ice, and strain into a rocks glass. Garnish with a half-slice of lemon. The origins of this drink would seem to lie in some unfathomable association of gentlemen of the press with a fondness for alcoholic liquor.

## GIMLET

**2 measures Plymouth gin**

**¾ measure lime cordial (traditionally Rose's)**

Stir together with ice in a tumbler and serve. Add a piece of lime peel if desired. This, the original gin and lime, was once made with equal parts gin and lime cordial, which would be a touch sugary for today's tastes.

## ORANGE BLOSSOM

From the original gin and lime to the original gin and orange: the Orange Blossom is simply equal parts (say, 1½ measures each) of gin and freshly squeezed orange juice, shaken with ice and strained into a cocktail glass. It is said that these were being consumed on the night of the scandalous drunken orgy that finished off the career of the silent comedian Fatty Arbuckle. You don't have to go that far, but do bother to shake the drink. It is nothing like a simple bar mixture of bottled orange juice added to gin in the glass. Nor is the spirit drowned. In those sweeter-toothed days, they used to add a pinch of sugar to it as well, but it isn't necessary.

## CLOVER CLUB

**2 measures gin**
**1 measure grenadine**
**juice of half a lemon**
**white of half an egg**

Shake very vigorously with ice, so as to ensure that the egg white is completely amalgamated. Strain into a tumbler, and garnish with lemon. This frothy pink cocktail was named after a group of intellectual glitterati who used to meet at a Philadelphia hotel in the days before Prohibition.

## LEAP YEAR

**2 measures gin**
**½ measure sweet red vermouth**
**½ measure Grand Marnier**
**dash lemon juice**

Shake with ice, and strain into a cocktail glass. Squeeze lemon peel over the surface. This was created by Harry Craddock at the Savoy during the Leap Year celebrations of 29 February 1928.

## STAR

**1½ measures gin**

**1½ measures calvados**

**dash sweet red vermouth**

**dash dry vermouth**

**1 tsp grapefruit juice**

Shake with ice, and strain into a cocktail glass. A number of cocktail recipes came to have this name, but this is in all probability the first, a strong, dry, sour mixture to whet the appetite for dinner.

## HI HO

**2 measures gin**

**1 measure white port**

**1 tsp orange bitters**

Shake with ice, and strain into a cocktail glass. Garnish with a twist of lemon peel. Created around 1930 in a Hollywood nightclub of the same name.

## BRONX

**1½ measures gin**

**¾ measure sweet red vermouth**

**¾ measure dry vermouth**

**juice of a quarter of an orange**

Shake with ice, and strain into a cocktail glass. Decorate with a twist of orange peel. Said to have been created at the long-vanished Big Brass Rail bar at the Waldorf Hotel, New York, in the early years of the twentieth century.

## MERRY WIDOW

**1½ measures gin**

**1 measure dry vermouth**

**1 tsp Bénédictine**

**1 tsp absinthe**

**dash Angostura bitters**

Stir with ice in a mixing jug and strain into a chilled cocktail glass. Squeeze a piece of lemon peel over the surface and then drop it into the drink. This cocktail was created in honour of a production of the Franz Lehár operetta of the same name that was being staged at the Savoy Theatre.

## DAMN THE WEATHER

**1 measure gin**

**½ measure sweet red vermouth**

**½ measure fresh orange juice**

**3 dashes orange curaçao**

Shake with ice, and strain into a cocktail glass or small wineglass. Garnish with a half-slice of orange. To be served on a wet summer's day.

## HARLEM

**1½ measures gin**

**1 measure maraschino**

**1 measure pineapple juice**

**3 pineapple chunks**

Using a muddler or pestle, crush the pineapple chunks in a small glass until they are reduced to a pasty consistency. Add these and the liquid ingredients to the shaker with plenty of ice, and shake thoroughly. Strain into a whisky tumbler. Garnish with another whole pineapple chunk on a cocktail stick. A delightful recipe that was served at the Cotton Club in the Harlem district of New York in the 1920s, in defiance of Prohibition.

## APPETISER

**1 measure gin**

**1 measure red Dubonnet**

**juice of half an orange**

Shake with ice, and strain into a cocktail glass. The drink's name indicates its function.

## POPPY

**2 measures gin**

**1 measure brown crème de cacao**

Shake with ice, and strain into a cocktail glass. A strong, all-alcohol mixture that might go down well at the end of a dinner.

## RESOLUTE

**1½ measures gin**

**¾ measure apricot brandy**

**¾ measure lemon juice**

Shake with ice, and strain into a cocktail glass. Add a twist of lemon peel.

## SILVER BULLET

**1 measure gin**

**½ measure kümmel**

**½ measure lemon juice**

Shake with ice, and strain into a small wineglass. Garnish with a half-slice of lemon.

The Great Depression and the coming of the Second World War accounted for the demise of the cocktail, and it was only in the period following the Allied victory that drinking once again assumed something like the adventurousness that it had had during the twenties.

## STORK CLUB COCKTAIL

**1½ measures gin**

**dash Cointreau**

**dash lime juice**

**dash Angostura bitters**

**juice of half an orange**

Shake with ice, and strain into a small wineglass. Add twists of orange and lime peel. This was the proprietary cocktail of New York's Stork Club, the recipe for which is included in the 1946 bar book compiled by its head bartender Lucius Beebe.

## STAY UP LATE

**2 measures gin**

**½ measure brandy**

**½ measure lemon juice**

**½ measure soda water**

**pinch of caster sugar**

Mix all the ingredients well with ice in a tall glass, and add a slice of lemon. This recipe, with its invitation to misbehave, is credited to Veronica, the hat-check girl at the Stork Club in the mid-1940s.

## EARTHQUAKE

**1 measure gin**

**1 measure bourbon whiskey**

**¾ measure absinthe**

Shake with ice, and strain into a cocktail glass. No garnish. This is a lethally destructive cocktail that will make the ground appear to tremble beneath your feet, as its name duly warns.

## ASTOR'S PAINLESS ANAESTHETIC

**3 measures gin**

**1 measure dry vermouth**

**1 measure sweet red vermouth**

**1 measure brandy**

**dash orange bitters**

**pinch of caster sugar**

Shake well with ice, and strain into a tall glass. This formidably strong recipe is credited to the film actress Mary Astor, whose greatest screen role came in *The Maltese Falcon* (1941).

## RED LION

**1½ measures gin**

**¾ measure Grand Marnier**

**¼ measure lemon juice**

**3 dashes grenadine**

Shake with ice, and strain into a cocktail glass. Garnish with a half-slice of lemon.

During the cocktail renaissance of the late 1970s and early 1980s, creamy concoctions were especially popular. They wrap the hit of alcohol in a velvet glove that makes them taste deceptively innocuous.

## ALEXANDER

**1½ measures gin**

**¾ measure brown crème de cacao**

**¾ measure double cream**

Shake well with ice, and strain into a cocktail glass. Shave a little dark chocolate over the surface of the drink. The elder sibling of the since much more famous Brandy Alexander (for which recipe, see the Brandy chapter).

## SILVER JUBILEE

**1 measure gin**

**1 measure crème de banane**

**1 measure double cream**

Shake well with ice, and strain into a cocktail glass. A cocktail invented to mark the occasion of Queen Elizabeth II's 25-year Jubilee in 1977.

## YELLOW FINGERS

**1 measure gin**

**1 measure crème de mûre**

**½ measure crème de banane**

**½ measure double cream**

Shake well with ice, and strain into a cocktail glass. This is a lighter-textured creamy cocktail with a pronounced fruity taste.

Multi-ingredient cocktails were very much in vogue in the eighties.

## SHANGHAI GIN FIZZ

**½ measure gin**

**½ measure yellow Chartreuse**

**½ measure Bénédictine**

**½ measure lemon juice**

**soda water to top up**

Shake the first four ingredients with ice, and strain into a highball glass. Top with chilled soda. Garnish with a half-slice of lemon and a cherry. Drink through straws.

## INCA

**1 measure gin**

**1 measure sweet red vermouth**

**1 measure dry vermouth**

**1 measure pale dry sherry**

**dash orgeat syrup**

**dash Angostura bitters**

Stir in a mixing jug with ice. Strain into a tumbler, and add a pineapple chunk and a cocktail cherry threaded together on a stick. Drink through straws.

The instruction to 'drink through straws' had become *de rigueur* by this stage. Not unknown during the first cocktail era, they were now as universal in bars as those silly little folding paper parasols were. A myth grew up at this time, presumably not unconnected with the cocktail craze, that drinking through straws accelerated the alcohol into one's system. This widely shared belief eventually led to the sight of grown men drinking export-strength lager through straws stuck in the top of the can.

Oddly enough, in the Victorian era exactly the opposite was believed to be the case, and with a sight more justification, as is outlined by the great nineteenth-century chef Charles Francatelli, who wrote: 'I am afraid that very genteel persons will be exceedingly shocked at the words ''suck through a straw'', but when I tell them that the very act of imbibition through a straw prevents the gluttonous absorption of large and baneful quantities of drink, they will, I make no doubt, accept the vulgar precept for the sake of its protection against sudden inebriety.'

## GLOOM RAISER

**2 measures gin**
**¼ measure dry vermouth**
**2 dashes Pernod**
**2 dashes grenadine**

Stir with ice in a mixing jug. Strain into a small wineglass and add a cocktail cherry. Should you wish to raise a little gloom, this recipe plays on gin's age-old (and mythical) reputation as the 'low spirit', the one likeliest to induce a bout of depression.

## LEO

**2 measures gin**

**1 measure Cointreau**

**½ measure lime juice**

**dash Pernod**

**dash green crème de menthe**

Shake with ice, and strain into a cocktail glass. Add a slice of lime.

Today's mixtures bear only a distant relation to the thunderously powerful concoctions of yesteryear. Flavours are built up to disguise the alcohol hit in many instances, while the proliferation of novelty ingredients has been a hallmark of the last decade or so. The Martini, in particular, has come in for some serious reinvention.

## CHOCOLATE NUT MARTINI

**1½ measures Plymouth gin**

**¾ measure white crème de cacao**

**¾ measure Frangelico**

Prepare a chilled martini (cocktail) glass by dipping the rim in sugar syrup, and then into freshly fine-ground coffee beans. Shake the alcohol ingredients with ice, and strain into the prepared glass.

## SALT-AND-PEPPER MARTINI

**2 measures gin**

**½ measure lemon juice**

**½ measure grapefruit juice**

**½ measure sugar syrup**

**2 dashes Angostura bitters**

Shake with ice, and strain into a martini glass that has been crusted with coarse sea salt.

## BLACK MARTINI

**2½ measures gin**

**½ measure crème de mûre**

Stir with ice in a mixing jug, and strain into a chilled martini glass. Garnish with a black olive on a stick. The proportions in this drink ensure that it has only the most discreet blackberry flavour from the liqueur.

## SMOKY MARTINI

**2½ measures Plymouth gin**

**dash of Laphroaig malt whisky**

Stir with ice in a mixing jug, and strain into a chilled martini glass. Add a twist of lemon rind. The name of this cocktail derives from the richly peaty, smoky flavour of Laphroaig, a single malt Scotch from the Islay region. It's the kind of drink that separates the men from the boys – or the women from the girls, for that matter. New York bartender Audrey Saunders rolls the ice with which the drink is mixed in Pernod before putting it in the jug, for that extra savoury kick.

## WINSTON MARTINI

**dash Frangelico**

**1 measure gin**

**1 measure spiced rum**

**dash lime cordial**

Dash the Frangelico into a mixing jug and then pour it out before putting the ice in. Add the other ingredients, stir well, and strain into a chilled martini glass. Add a twist of lemon. This was invented in the restaurant bar of one of the World Trade Centre towers that were destroyed in 2001.

Many of today's favourite compounds involve blending different fruit-juice flavours on a single alcohol base. This gin variation on the classic Sea Breeze (for which, see the vodka chapter) is very much in that mould.

## JUNIPER BREEZE

**2 measures Plymouth gin**

**½ measure elderflower cordial**

**1 measure grapefruit juice**

**½ measure cranberry juice**

**½ measure lime juice**

Add the ingredients in this order to a large whisky tumbler filled with cracked ice, stir to blend, and garnish with a slice of lime and a grapefruit twist.

Here is a recipe from cocktail author Robert Cross that uses the traditional Dutch product.

## STRIKE'S ON

**2 measures Oude (Old) Genever**

**½ measure lemon juice**

**½ measure pineapple syrup (from a can of fruit)**

**1½ measures sparkling apple juice (Appletise, etc.)**

Shake the first three ingredients with ice, and strain into a tumbler loaded with cracked ice. Add the fizzy apple juice, and garnish with a half-slice of lemon. Quite which strike this drink commemorates isn't clear, but it looks like a good excuse to down tools in any event.

## HONOLULU SHOOTER

**1 measure gin**

**1 tsp pineapple juice**

**1 tsp orange juice**

**1 tsp lemon juice**

**1 tsp pineapple syrup**

**1 drop Angostura bitters**

Shake with ice, and strain into a chilled shot glass. Down in one.

## BLACKOUT

**1 measure gin**

**½ measure crème de mûre**

**¼ measure lime juice**

**¼ measure sugar syrup**

Shake with ice, and strain into a chilled shot glass. Down in one. A cocktail with which to say, 'Thank you and goodnight.'

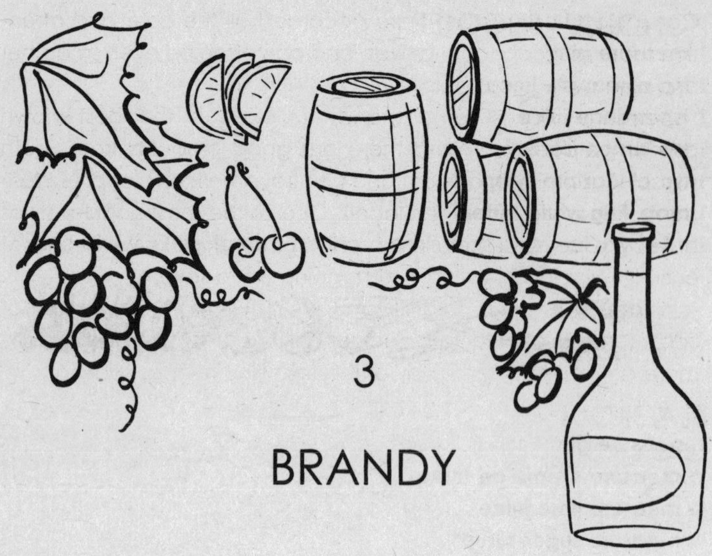

# 3

# BRANDY

Purists who relish warming a fine old cognac in a brandy balloon in the hand after dinner may recoil in horror at the thought of shaking it up with ice and other potions for a cocktail session. The fact is, though, that brandy makes an excellent mixed drink base, and even though you wouldn't necessarily want to use finest XO Napoleon in the shaker, neither should you use the cheapest you can lay your hands on. Anything from France labelled 'brandy', as distinct from cognac or armagnac, should be left on the shelf. One taste of it neat will soon demonstrate why.

Cognac and armagnac are the premier league of world brandy, the former from the Charentes region of western France, the latter from further south in Gascony. They are quite different in style, with armagnac having a noticeably more aromatic, even floral, scent to it. It tends to be cheaper than cognac too. The big names in cognac – Martell, Rémy-Martin, Hine, Hennessy, Courvoisier – are the aristocracy, and their top grades, VSOP and XO, are cask-aged for many years.

After France, the next best source of brandy is Spain, where the spirit is made in the sherry region (as Brandy de Jérez) and in

Catalonia. These products are accorded all the care and attention that finest cognac receives, and can often be even smoother and mellower on the palate.

Germany makes some brandy (Asbach is the best-known brand), as does Italy, and there are good products from South Africa, California, and South and Central America (Mexico's Presidente is a world-renowned label). One of the most singular styles of all is Greece's Metaxa, a lush, toffeeish potion with a not entirely reliable star-rating system going up to seven.

Whatever its origin, brandy imparts a full-throttle undertow of rich, rounded intensity to a cocktail mixture, and it is consequently more advisable to serve any of the following recipes sparingly.

## BRANDY SMASH

**1½ measures brandy**

**four mint leaves**

**½ measure sugar syrup, or 1 tsp caster sugar**

Using a muddler or pestle, grind the mint leaves into the sugar or sugar syrup until a rough green paste is formed. Add plenty of smashed ice to a tumbler, add the ground mint and brandy, and stir. Squeeze lemon peel over the top, and garnish with a cherry. This is a mid-nineteenth century American formula that could also be made with whisky, gin or white rum instead of the brandy. Made with whisky and turned into a long drink with soda, it became the now better-known Mint Julep (see whisky chapter).

## B&B

This dead simple, but abidingly popular, recipe consists simply of equal measures of brandy (use a good cognac) and Bénédictine, poured in that order into a balloon glass, swirled and drunk. These days, it is often pre-stirred with ice in a jug before being strained into the glass, but this is not quite traditional. B&B should be a warming potion, best served after dinner.

## BRANDY ALEXANDER

**1 measure cognac**

**1 measure brown crème de cacao**

**1 measure double cream**

Shake well with ice, and strain into a cocktail glass. Grate some dark chocolate or nutmeg over the surface. This is certainly not the oldest, but probably the best-loved, cream cocktail of them all. It is a whole lot more enjoyable than proprietary cream liqueurs, and – despite what you may hear – tastes nothing at all like Bailey's.

## DEPTH BOMB

**1½ measures brandy**

**1½ measures calvados**

**4 dashes grenadine**

**1 dash lemon juice**

Shake with ice, and strain into a cocktail glass. Garnish with a half-slice of lemon. This cocktail is one of several to take its name from First World War munitions, and is a suitably explosive mix. (There was another, gin-based, cocktail called Depth Charge, which is sometimes understandably confused with this one.)

## BRANDY FIX

**2 measures brandy**

**1 measure cherry brandy**

**1 tsp sugar syrup**

**juice of half a lemon**

Pack a tumbler with finely shaved ice, add the ingredients and stir. Add the squeezed-out shell of the lemon to the drink, and serve with straws. The Fix dates from the first half of the nineteenth century, and was always a fruity drink. When fruit-flavoured syrups became commercially available, they were used instead of plain sugar syrup and by the 1920s a fruit-flavoured liqueur was being used as well, as here. Gin Fix was a popular variation.

## THE CLASSIC COCKTAIL

**1½ measures brandy**

**½ measure maraschino**

**½ measure orange curaçao**

**½ measure lemon juice**

Moisten the rim of a cocktail glass, and dip it in caster sugar to frost the rim. Shake the ingredients with ice, and strain into the prepared glass. Squeeze lemon peel over the top. This is a delightful cocktail from the 1920s, and fully worthy of its authoritative name.

## SIDECAR

**1½ measures brandy**

**¾ measure Cointreau**

**¾ measure lemon juice**

Shake with ice, and strain into a small tumbler or rocks glass. This recipe was created at Harry's Bar in Paris, around 1920. Some recipes use equal measures of the three components, which results in a stronger and sourer mixture, but both *The Savoy Cocktail Book* and Ambrose Heath's *Good Drinks* (1939) show these proportions. It is a surprisingly heavy-tasting cocktail, although a good one, and can be leavened by having a little shaved ice served in it.

## CORPSE REVIVER

**1½ measures brandy**

**¾ measure calvados**

**¾ measure sweet red vermouth**

Shake with ice, and strain into a cocktail glass. Harry Craddock at the Savoy recommended this before eleven in the morning, 'or whenever steam and energy are needed'. The era was cheerfully sanguine about the consequences of over-indulging, and threw up many instances of cocktails with a pseudo-medicinal bent to them. Nowadays, we would tend to be more circumspect about addressing any ailment with an ingestion of strong alcohol.

Here is another 'Reviver', this one for the clapped-out digestive system.

## STOMACH REVIVER

**1 measure brandy**

**1 measure kümmel**

**¼ measure Fernet Branca**

**½ tsp Angostura bitters**

Shake with ice, and strain into a shot-glass. Knock back. If the cocktail doesn't seem to have worked after ten minutes, resist the temptation to try a second.

## BOOSTER

**2 measures brandy**

**½ measure orange curaçao**

**white of half an egg, whisked until gently frothy**

Shake well with ice, and strain into a small wineglass. Sprinkle ground nutmeg on the surface. Another allegedly reviving drink that may (or may not) be just what the doctor ordered.

## HARRY'S PICK-ME-UP

**1 measure brandy**

**1 tsp grenadine**

**juice of half a lemon**

**brut champagne**

Shake the first three ingredients with ice, and strain into a champagne flute. Top up with the champagne. As therapeutic drinks go, this – Mr Craddock's own formula – is much more like it.

## VANDERBILT

**1½ measures fine cognac**

**½ measure cherry brandy**

**3 dashes sugar syrup**

**2 dashes Angostura bitters**

Shake with ice, and strain into a cocktail glass. Garnish with a cocktail cherry and a twist of lemon. The Vanderbilt for whom this drink was created in 1912 was Cornelius of that ilk.

## THUNDERCLAP

**1 measure brandy**

**1 measure whisky**

**1 measure gin**

Shake with ice, and strain into a cocktail glass. There are a number of recipes of the early twentieth century that look like adolescent experiments gone wrong in today's more sophisticated era, and this is pretty much one of them. It is ragingly unpleasant, a complete mishmash of ill-assorted tastes, but perhaps worth trying once for its period interest. Harry Craddock suggests making it in sufficient quantity to cater for half-a-dozen people. Serve it bravely, he counsels, and then 'run for your life'.

## OLYMPIC

**1 measure brandy**

**1 measure orange curaçao**

**1 measure freshly squeezed orange juice**

Shake with ice, and strain into a cocktail glass. Decorate with a twist of orange rind. Created in honour of the 1924 Olympic Games, held in Paris.

## STINGER

The Stinger, which dates from around the time of the Great War, is a two-to-one mixture of any base spirit with the white version of crème de menthe. The classic Stinger is made with brandy (two measures to one of crème de menthe), which is why we include it here, but either whisky or dark rum make acceptable bases too. Originally, the two ingredients were simply poured straight into the glass, swirled and downed, but time came to refine it into a shaken drink to be served in a cocktail glass filled with crushed ice (in effect, a *frappé*). The effect of a Stinger is a little like having brushed one's teeth with something rather fierce.

## EAST INDIA

**1½ measures brandy**

**1 measure orange curaçao**

**1 measure pineapple juice**

**dash Angostura bitters**

Stir the ingredients with ice in a mixing jug, and then strain into a tumbler. Garnish with a half-slice of orange. Contemporary cocktail king Dale Degroff thought he had invented this for the millennium celebrations, using a special bottling of Courvoisier cognac, but confesses to a moment of serendipity on discovering it under this name in a book of 1946. (You'll also find it in your copy of *The Savoy Cocktail Book*, Dale.)

## MIKADO

**2 measures cognac**

**1 tsp orange curaçao**

**1 tsp amaretto**

**1 tsp crème de noyau**

**2 dashes Angostura bitters**

Shake with ice, and strain into a cocktail glass. A production of the Gilbert and Sullivan operetta of the same name was running at the Savoy Theatre when this cocktail was created in the hotel's American Bar. We have used amaretto liqueur in place of the original (almondy-tasting) orgeat syrup, which isn't easily come by.

## HARVARD

**1½ measures brandy**

**1½ measures sweet red vermouth**

**2 dashes Angostura bitters**

**¼ measure grenadine**

**¼ measure lemon juice**

Shake with ice, and strain into a small tumbler. Decorate with a twist of lemon. A drink created at Harvard University in the 1920s to deflect the conscientious from their studies.

## YOUNG MAN

**1½ measures brandy**

**½ measure sweet red vermouth**

**2 dashes orange curaçao**

**dash Angostura bitters**

Shake with ice, and strain into a small tumbler. Add a stuffed olive. This is a little like the Harvard, only less sweet.

## PRESTO

**2 measures brandy**

**½ measure sweet red vermouth**

**½ measure fresh orange juice**

**dash absinthe**

Shake with ice, and strain into a cocktail glass. Garnish with a piece of orange peel.

Moving into the 1930s and 40s, we find brandy used a little less in the cocktail repertoire than it had been. Perhaps the feeling that it was best drunk on its own was beginning to take hold.

## BRANDY ZOOM

**2 measures cognac**

**¾ measure whipping cream**

**1 tsp clear honey**

**1 measure hot water**

Dissolve the honey in the hot water, and then shake it with the other ingredients with plenty of ice to cool down the hot water. Strain into a cocktail glass. The Zoom enjoyed a brief craze in the 1930s, and was a generic mixture that could also be made with bourbon, dark rum or (less successfully) gin instead of brandy. There is a faint hint of the hot toddy about it, not quite the sort of thing to get a party started, which perhaps explains why it soon 'zoomed' off the radar.

## FOXHOUND

**1 measure brandy**

**½ measure cranberry juice**

**¼ measure kümmel**

**dash lemon juice**

Shake with ice, and strain into a small tumbler. Garnish with a half-slice of lemon. This is an English cocktail recipe once favoured by the huntin', shootin' and fishin' set.

## KISS THE BOYS GOODBYE

**1 measure brandy**

**1 measure sloe gin**

**1 tsp lemon juice**

**white of half an egg**

Shake with ice, and strain into a tumbler containing cracked ice and a slice of lemon. This drink was invented as a toast to American soldiers departing for Europe to fight in the Second World War.

## POLONAISE

**1 measure brandy**

**½ measure dark rum**

**½ measure pale dry sherry**

**½ measure lemon juice**

**½ measure grenadine**

**2 dashes Angostura bitters**

Shake with ice, and strain into a cocktail glass. Garnish with a twist of lemon. This rather dry and bracing cocktail sounds as though it ought to have Polish vodka in it, but it doesn't. There isn't necessarily any logic to traditional cocktail names.

## DEBUTANTE'S DREAM

**½ measure brandy**
**½ measure bourbon**
**½ measure fresh orange juice**
**dash lemon juice**

Shake with ice, and strain into a cocktail glass. Decorate with orange and lemon twists. The modest quantity of alcohol in this drink was thought suitable for a young lady just emerging on to the social scene.

The 1970s and 80s used brandy as the bass-note in highly fruity or creamy mixtures, where it adds a touch of gravitas amid the surrounding frivolity.

## DIZZY DAME

**1 measure brandy**
**¾ measure Tia Maria**
**½ measure cherry brandy**
**1 measure double cream**

Shake well with ice, and strain into a cocktail glass. Balance a cocktail stick with a cherry speared on it across the rim of the glass. The expected clash of cherry and coffee flavours fails to materialise in the finished product, which is all mellifluous harmony.

## BRANDY HUM

Swirl equal measures of cognac and Van der Hum liqueur with ice in a balloon glass. A fruitier version of B&B.

And while you have the Van der Hum to hand:

## SUNDOWNER

**1 measure South African brandy**

**¼ measure Van der Hum liqueur**

**¼ measure lemon juice**

**¼ measure orange juice**

Shake with ice, and strain into a cocktail glass. Decorate with half-slices of orange and lemon.

## BAYOU

**1½ measures brandy**

**½ measure peach brandy**

**1 measure peach juice**

**½ measure lime juice**

Shake with roughly cracked ice, and pour (ice included) into a tumbler or rocks glass. Garnish with a slice of ripe peach.

## TORPEDO

**2 measures brandy**

**1 measure Kahlua**

**½ measure egg white**

Shake well with ice, and strain into a tumbler of cracked ice. There are various other cocktails with the same name, mostly having the same kind of alcohol charge as this one has.

## CUMPARASITA

**1 measure brandy**
**1 measure apricot brandy**
**1 measure fresh orange juice**
**¼ measure kirsch**
**¼ measure dry vermouth**
**1 measure double cream**
**dash grenadine**

Shake all but the last ingredient well with ice, and strain into a tall narrow glass half-filled with ice. Add the grenadine dash and watch it sink through the cocktail, before very gently swirling it with a long spoon.

## MONTMARTRE

**1 measure brandy**
**½ measure yellow Chartreuse**
**dash lemon juice**
**dash Angostura bitters**
**champagne to top up**

Shake the first four ingredients with ice, and strain into a champagne flute. Top with champagne. Add a cocktail cherry, and drink through a straw. An inimitably Gallic experience, this one.

## NEVER ON SUNDAY

**1 measure Metaxa**
**½ measure ouzo**
**dash Angostura bitters**
**dash lemon juice**
**ginger beer and champagne to top up**

Mix the first four ingredients with ice in a jug, and strain into a champagne flute. Top with a 50–50 mix of ginger beer and champagne. Drop a piece of crystallised ginger into the drink. A recipe, from Michael Walker's cocktail book of 1980, to help you use up those holiday souvenir bottles still lurking at the back of the cupboard.

## POMPEII

**1 measure brandy**

**½ measure white crème de cacao**

**½ measure amaretto**

**1 measure double cream**

Shake well with ice, and strain into a cocktail glass (better still, a champagne saucer, if you have one to hand). Sprinkle untoasted flaked almonds over the surface.

## GRANADA

**1 measure brandy**

**1 measure pale dry sherry**

**½ measure orange curaçao**

**tonic water to top up**

Stir the first three ingredients with ice in a mixing jug, and strain into a highball glass. Top up with Schweppes Indian tonic water. Add a half-slice of orange, and drink through straws.

## AMBIENCE

**1 measure Hennessy VSOP cognac**

**1 measure vodka**

**¼ measure Mandarine Napoléon**

**4 measures fresh orange juice**

**1 measure lime juice**

**1 tsp sugar syrup**

Frost the rim of a tall glass by dipping it in lime juice and then caster sugar, and half-fill it with cracked ice. Shake all the ingredients with ice, and strain into the prepared glass. Garnish with a slice of lime and a cherry skewered on a cocktail stick. Drink through straws. This recipe was conceived by the Hennessy cognac house.

## AMERICAN BEAUTY

**1 measure brandy**

**1 measure dry vermouth**

**1 measure fresh orange juice**

**2 dashes grenadine**

**2 dashes sugar syrup**

**½ measure ruby port**

Shake the first five ingredients with ice, and strain into a cocktail glass. Pour the port carefully over the top, so that it floats in a red slick. Garnish further with a pink rose petal. This drink is named after a variety of rose, one familiar to anybody who has seen the film of the same name. Hence the garnish.

Brandy holds its own in those of today's popular mixtures that include it. Try experimenting with brandies from countries other than France in the recipes that follow.

## BRANDY MELBA

**1½ measures brandy**
**½ measure peach schnapps**
**¼ measure crème de framboise**
**½ measure lemon juice**
**dash orange bitters**

Shake with ice, and strain into a cocktail glass. Decorate with a wedge of peach and a couple of raspberries. The inspiration for this mixture is the classic dessert, Peach Melba, in which the peach is served with ice-cream and a raspberry coulis. If you can't find orange bitters, substitute a dash of curaçao instead.

## BACCHUS

**2 measures brandy**
**1 measure apricot brandy**
**1 measure lime juice**

Stir in a mixing jug with ice, and strain into a tumbler half-filled with cracked ice. Garnish with a slice of lime.

## COFFEE BREAK

**½ measure brandy**
**½ measure Kahlua**
**hot coffee to top up**
**1 dsp whipped cream**

Pour the two alcohols into a tall glass containing a spoon to conduct heat. Fill up with strong hot black cafetière coffee, and float the cream on top. This is an altogether more appealing prospect than the traditional Irish coffee.

## MAN OVERBOARD

**1 measure brandy**

**¾ measure Cointreau**

**½ measure Galliano**

**½ measure grenadine**

Shake with ice, and strain into a cocktail glass. Add a cherry on a stick.

## FRENCH BITE

**1 measure brandy**

**¾ measure Mandarine Napoléon**

**2 measures sparkling apple juice (such as Appletise)**

Add the ingredients in this order to a small tumbler half-filled with cracked ice, and give the drink a quick stir.

## TONIGHT'S THE NIGHT

**1½ measures brandy**

**½ measure sweet red vermouth**

**½ measure passion-fruit syrup**

Shake with plenty of cracked ice, and pour, including the ice, into a tumbler or rocks glass. Flavoured syrups are increasingly available, but if you can't find the passion-fruit version, use a mixture of juice from a fresh fruit with a little plain sugar syrup instead.

## ROUND-UP

**1 measure brandy**

**1 measure white crème de cacao**

**¾ measure crème de banane**

**½ measure white crème de menthe**

**1 measure 7-UP**

Shake the first four ingredients with ice, and strain into a small wineglass. Add the measure of 7-UP. This potion, from a cocktail guide by Robert Cross, is an intensely sweet, even rather vulgar mixture, but delicious with it. It seems to represent a 'round-up' of the most obviously appealing liqueur flavours – mint, banana and chocolate.

## HAPPY HONEY

**2 measures brandy**

**1 measure grapefruit juice**

**2 tsp clear honey**

Shake well with ice, and strain into a cocktail glass. A clever balance of sweet and sharp flavours.

## INTERNATIONAL STINGER

**2 measures Metaxa**

**1 measure Galliano**

Shake with ice, and serve on the rocks in a small tumbler. This is nothing like a classic Stinger (qv), but is worth trying anyway for its peculiar, aromatic potency.

## GOATHERD

**1 measure brandy**

**½ measure kirsch**

**½ measure cherry brandy**

**1 tsp amaretto**

**1 measure double cream**

Shake well with ice, and strain into a cocktail glass. Garnish with a cherry on a stick. The logic behind the name of this creamy concoction momentarily escapes us.

## SEVEN DIALS

**1 measure brandy**

**1 measure brown crème de cacao**

**1 tsp Grand Marnier**

**1 measure double cream**

**1 egg yolk**

Shake all the ingredients very briskly with ice to amalgamate the egg, and strain into a tumbler half-filled with cracked ice. Be sure your egg is free-range and very fresh.

## LEMON LADY

**1 measure brandy**

**½ measure Cointreau**

**3 measures part-melted lemon sorbet**

Shake well and strain into a pre-chilled cocktail glass. Garnish with a couple of half-slices of lemon. As you are using a frozen ingredient in this recipe already, there is no need to add ice to the shaker.

Using sorbets and ice-creams in cocktails is very much the mood of the moment. Here is another such:

## FRENCH ALPS

**1 measure brandy**

**1 measure Mandarine Napoléon**

**2 tbsps vanilla ice-cream**

Add the ingredients to an electric blender, and whizz them up for a few seconds. Pour into a chilled cocktail glass, and garnish with a sprinkling of grated orange zest.

## RIVIERA

**1½ measures brandy**

**1½ measures brown crème de cacao**

**½ measure Punt e Mes (or Dubonnet)**

**¾ measure Kahlua**

**1 dsp whipped double cream**

Shake the first four ingredients with ice, and strain into a tall narrow glass. Spoon the cream on top, and grate a piece of dark chocolate over it.

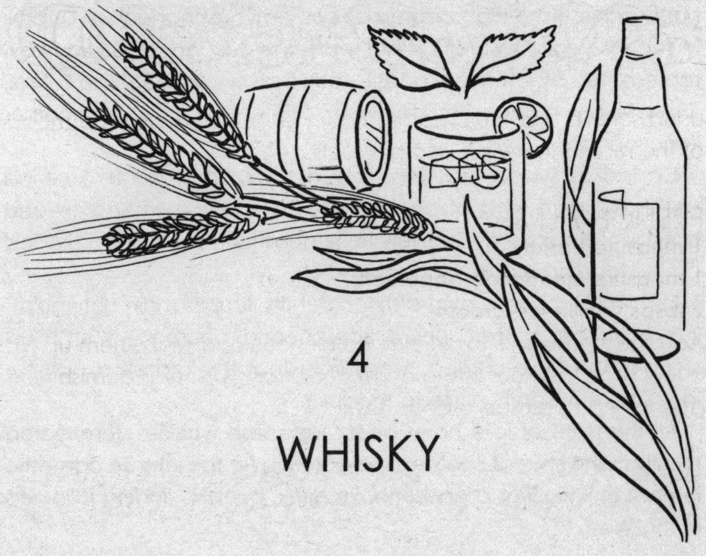

# 4

# WHISKY

Undoubtedly the greatest of the grain distillates, whisky – or whiskey, depending on where it comes from – is made all over the world, with each producing country and region having its own preferred style. It can be made from barley, rye or maize (the last is known as 'corn' in the Americas), or a combination of grains, and given a wide range of different treatments after the distillation process is complete.

Pre-eminent among the world's whiskies is Scotch, a stylistically unique product that has been much imitated, but the flavour of which has never been precisely reproduced anywhere else. At the top of the quality tree are the single malts, unblended whiskies produced from the base produce of a single distillery, but inexpensive blended Scotch is a thoroughly reliable product too, quite unlike cheap brandy or rum.

Coming up on the inside track in worldwide popularity is the American whiskey known as bourbon, produced in the state of Kentucky. Bourbon is a richer, sweeter style of whiskey made from at least 51% corn, and matured in charred wooden barrels. Its many famous brands, including Jim Beam and Maker's Mark, have achieved a high degree of consumer recognition in Europe in recent years. As well as bourbon, there is Tennessee whiskey, represented by just two brands – Jack Daniel's and George Dickel. Rye whiskey, made with a minimum 51% of that cereal, is another American style.

Canadian whisky has long been popular in North America generally, as a kind of compromise style between Scotch and bourbon. It has an attractively fruity quality on the palate, typified by the leading brand, Canadian Club.

Irish whiskey has its own distinct identity too, its main distinguishing point being that, unlike Scotch and bourbon, it isn't just double- but triple-distilled. Many insist that this imparts a particularly soft, enveloping style to the spirit.

All the rage of late have been Japanese whiskies, formulated mostly in the style of Scotch, and catering for the intense domestic interest in whisky as a gastronomic drink, but also finding followers in the West.

One of the oldest cocktails in this book, having originated in the Southern States of the USA in the eighteenth century, the Julep was (and still is) traditionally drunk on Kentucky Derby Day, the first Saturday in May.

## MINT JULEP

**2 measures bourbon**

**1 tbsp hot water**

**7–8 fresh spearmint leaves**

**1 tbsp caster sugar**

Grind the torn-up mint leaves with the sugar in a pestle and mortar (or otherwise with a muddler in a mixing jug), adding the hot water to assist in releasing the minty juices. Empty this mixture into a tall glass half-filled with crushed ice, followed by the bourbon. Stir well until the outside of the glass has frosted up, and the ice has just begun to dilute the drink a little. Sing as you go. This is a merry cocktail that marks the start of the drinking season.

## WHISKY SOUR

**2 measures bourbon (or Scotch, if you prefer)**

**juice of half a lemon**

**1 tsp caster sugar**

Mix the sugar and lemon juice in a small rocks glass with a few bits of broken ice. Add the whisky. Of all the basic sour recipes, this and the classic Daiquiri (qv) are incomparably the finest.

One of the world's most famous cocktails is the Manhattan, reportedly invented at the club of that name in New York City in the 1870s for Jennie Churchill, Winston's mother. It should ideally be made with rye, as that was then the whiskey of choice in that environ, but is also good with bourbon or Tennessee whiskey.

## MANHATTAN

**2 measures rye whiskey**

**¼ measure dry vermouth**

**¼ measure sweet red vermouth**

Mix well with ice in a jug until the drink is very cold, and then strain into a small tumbler. Drop a piece of lemon peel and a cocktail cherry into the drink. This formula, technically known as the Perfect Manhattan, mixes the two styles of vermouth. It can also be made with a half-measure of sweet red, or (less widely) with a half-measure of dry white, vermouth. Many recipes add a dash or two of Angostura bitters too, but the drink won't be bereft without it.

## OLD-FASHIONED

**2 measures bourbon**

**2 dashes Angostura bitters**

**1 tsp caster sugar**

Mix all the ingredients in a small tumbler very thoroughly, along with cracked ice, a slice of orange and a cherry, until the sugar is completely dissolved. This is an old Kentucky cocktail that is little more than a slightly sweetened, modified whiskey. At the Exhibit Bar in Balham, south London, where this drink is expertly prepared, a bartender of uncommon talents vouchsafed to the authors that a good Old-Fashioned should take precisely six minutes to prepare. At the end of this prescribed time, he held the glass up to the light, inviting us to peer through its base. This we duly did, and discovered that not a single grain of undissolved sugar remained. Had we been wearing hats at the time, we would unhesitatingly have taken them off to him.

One of the earliest performance drinks, the Blue Blazer was created by the great nineteenth-century master, Jerry Thomas. It is an insanely dangerous idea for the amateur, and is perhaps best tried outdoors, while wearing flame-retardant clothing, and having a fire extinguisher to hand, as well as somebody to call out the fire brigade, should you happen to ignite your eyebrows.

## BLUE BLAZER

**2 measures warmed Scotch**

**2 measures boiled water, plus some for warming the mugs**

**1 tsp sugar syrup**

**dash lemon juice**

Prepare a heatproof glass by adding the syrup and lemon juice to it, but no ice. Warm up two small earthenware mugs by swilling them with boiled water and pouring it out. Warm the Scotch in a small pan over gentle heat for a few seconds, and then add it to one of the mugs, adding a measure of boiled water to the other.

Using a long-stemmed match, set the Scotch alight, and pour it into the other mug. Continue pouring the flaming drink backwards and forwards between the two mugs, to demonstrate the flaring blue flame to your astonished onlookers, before tipping it into the heatproof glass. Add a piece of lemon peel.

## IRISH COCKTAIL

**2 measures Irish whiskey**

**2 dashes absinthe**

**2 dashes orange curaçao**

**1 dash maraschino**

**1 dash Angostura bitters**

Shake with ice, and strain into a cocktail glass. Squeeze a piece of orange peel over the surface, and then drop in a stuffed olive. This, and the following, were two of the earliest mixtures specifically created for Irish whiskey.

## SHAMROCK

**1 measure Irish whiskey**

**1 measure dry vermouth**

**¼ measure green Chartreuse**

**¼ measure green crème de menthe**

Shake with ice, and strain into a cocktail glass. Add a green olive on a stick. A 1920s recipe that could be served on St Patrick's Day (March 17), but not in any great quantity.

## AFFINITY

**1 measure Scotch**

**1 measure dry vermouth**

**1 measure sweet red vermouth**

**2 dashes Angostura bitters**

Stir well with ice in a mixing jug, and then strain into a small tumbler with a couple of ice-cubes in it. Squeeze a bit of lemon peel over the drink, and drop it in.

## ROB ROY

**1½ measures Scotch**

**1½ measures sweet red vermouth**

**dash Angostura bitters**

Shake with ice, and strain into a cocktail glass. This is a very slightly sweeter version of the recipe above, but was an annual hit at the Savoy bar in the 1920s, every St Andrew's Day (November 30).

## BOBBY BURNS

**1½ measures Scotch**

**1½ measures sweet red vermouth**

**¼ measure Bénédictine**

Shake with ice, and strain into a cocktail glass. Squeeze a piece of lemon peel over the drink, and drop it in. Another small variation on the Scotch-and-vermouth formula, but Harry Craddock reckoned that this was one of the best whisky cocktails, and we do not dissent.

## NEW YORK

**2 measures Canadian whisky**

**juice of half a lime *or* a quarter of a lemon**

**2 dashes grenadine**

**1 tsp caster sugar**

Shake well with ice, and strain into a cocktail glass. Garnish with a twist of orange.

## ORIENTAL COCKTAIL

**1½ measures rye whiskey**

**¾ measure sweet red vermouth**

**¾ measure white curaçao (or Cointreau)**

**juice of half a lime**

Shake with ice, and strain into a cocktail glass. Garnish with a slice of lime. This recipe was said to have been donated in 1924 by an American engineer working in the Philippines to a doctor who cured him of a potentially life-threatening fever.

## SAZERAC

**2 measures rye or Canadian whisky**

**dash absinthe**

**dash Angostura bitters**

**1 tsp sugar**

Stir with ice in a mixing jug, and pour without straining into a small tumbler. Squeeze a piece of lemon peel on the surface, and drop it in. This is an old southern American drink, much favoured in New Orleans.

## IRISH COFFEE

**2 measures Irish whiskey**
**1–2 tsps demerara sugar**
**freshly made black coffee to top up**
**whipped cream**

Using a heatproof glass (there is a tall, thick glass known as an Irish coffee glass, expressly for this purpose), mix the whiskey and sugar, before topping up with hot coffee. The traditional finish is to pour a layer of whipping cream carefully over the back of a dessert-spoon, so that it floats in a layer on the top of the drink. An easier, and rather more luxurious, recourse is to add a spoonful of softly whipped cream to it. A much-loved way of finishing a grand dinner that can famously be adapted to include almost any spirit or liqueur instead of the whiskey, but this is the original.

## RUSTY NAIL

**1½ measures Scotch**
**1½ measures Drambuie**

Add both ingredients to a tumbler packed with cracked ice, and stir. An inimitably Scottish cocktail that has deservedly become a classic.

And while we're on the subject:

## LOCH LOMOND

**1½ measures Scotch**
**¼ measure sugar syrup**
**2 dashes Angostura bitters**

Shake with ice, and strain into a cocktail glass. Squeeze a bit of lemon peel over the drink. As the attentive will note, this is a Scotched-up version of the Old-Fashioned, but shaken, not stirred.

Scotch whisky features more than any other spirit in drinks devised as cold remedies. They don't necessarily work. They just famously make you feel better, largely because alcohol goes to the head a lot more easily when one is under the weather.

## HOT TODDY

**1 measure Scotch**
**1 tsp clear honey**
**1 measure lemon juice**
**hot water to top up**

Mix the first three ingredients together in a small mug, and top with hot water, stirring to dissolve the honey.

## WHISKY MAC

**1½ measures Scotch**
**1½ measures green ginger wine (traditionally Crabbie's)**

Mix the two ingredients in a tumbler, and drink. As this is such an appealing mixture, you may not want to wait until you are ill before you try it, in which case, serve it with a couple of ice-cubes in it.

## BARBARY

**1 measure Scotch**

**1 measure gin**

**1 measure brown crème de cacao**

**¾ measure whipping cream**

Shake well with ice, and strain into a goblet-style wineglass. Dust with nutmeg. Whisky is not much used in cream cocktails, but this is a rather delightful one, from the bar list of the Stork Club in New York in the 1940s. Below is another.

## KICKING COW

**1 measure bourbon or rye**

**1 measure maple syrup**

**1 measure double cream**

Shake well with ice, and strain into a cocktail glass filled with crushed ice. A drink to pile on the calories.

## WILDFLOWER

**2 measures Scotch**

**1½ measures grapefuit juice**

**dash grenadine**

Add the ingredients in this order to a champagne flute that has been filled up with crushed ice and garnished with a twist of grapefruit peel.

## BOOMERANG

**1 measure rye whiskey**

**¾ measure dry vermouth**

**¾ measure Swedish punch**

**2 dashes lemon juice**

**1 dash Angostura bitters**

Stir with ice in a mixing jug, and strain into a wineglass. Garnish with a half-slice of lemon.

## WARD EIGHT

**2 measures rye whiskey**

**juice of half a lemon**

**¼ measure grenadine**

Shake with ice, and strain into a tumbler loaded with cracked ice, slices of orange and lemon, and a cherry. This was named not after a hospital room, but after one of the political divisions of the city of Boston, Massachusetts, the city where it was first served.

## COMMANDO

**1½ measures bourbon**

**¾ measure Cointreau**

**2 dashes Pernod**

**juice of half a lime**

Shake with ice, and strain into a cocktail glass. Garnish with a slice of lime.

## COTILLION

**1½ measures bourbon**
**½ measure Cointreau**
**½ measure orange juice**
**½ measure lemon juice**
**1 tsp overproof dark rum**

Shake the first four ingredients with ice, and strain into a cocktail glass. Float the dash of rum on the surface of the drink. One or two of these should set you up nicely for engaging in the French dance after which the drink is named.

## CHURCHILL

**1½ measures Scotch**
**½ measure sweet red vermouth**
**½ measure Cointreau**
**½ measure lime juice**

Shake with ice, and strain into a cocktail glass. Garnish with a slice of lime. The British wartime leader was honoured by this appropriately rousing cocktail, created at the Savoy.

Whisky got absorbed in a slightly awkward way when the cocktail revival of the 1970s and 1980s came round, often seeming to argue with the other ingredients in a mixture, rather than blending with them. Here are a few of the better recipes:

## SCOTCH SOLACE

**1 measure Scotch**

**½ measure Cointreau**

**1 tsp clear honey**

**15cl/¼ pint whole milk**

**1 measure double cream**

Shake well with ice, and strain into a highball glass. Decorate with a sprinkling of grated orange zest.

## TRINITY

**1 measure rye whiskey**

**1 measure dry vermouth**

**dash orange bitters**

**dash white crème de menthe**

**dash lime juice**

Shake with ice, and strain into a cocktail glass. Add a twist of lemon.

## PINK ALMOND

**1 measure Scotch**

**½ measure crème de noyau**

**½ measure kirsch**

**½ measure orgeat syrup (or amaretto)**

**½ measure lemon juice**

Shake with ice, and strain into a tumbler with a couple of cubes of ice. Add a half-slice of lemon.

## PRINCE EDWARD

**1 measure Scotch**

**½ measure dry vermouth**

**¼ measure Drambuie**

**soda water to top up**

Shake the first three ingredients with ice, and strain into a tall glass. Top with soda. Garnish with a half-slice of orange and a cocktail cherry on a stick.

## BLOOD AND SAND

**½ measure Scotch**

**½ measure cherry brandy**

**½ measure sweet red vermouth**

**½ measure orange juice**

Shake with ice, and strain into a cocktail glass. Decorate with a twist of orange peel.

## EMBASSY ROYAL

**1 measure bourbon**

**1 measure Drambuie**

**1 measure sweet red vermouth**

**2 dashes orange juice**

Shake with ice, and strain into a cocktail glass. Garnish with a twist of orange peel.

## SERPENT'S TOOTH

**1 measure Irish whiskey**

**2 measures sweet red vermouth**

**½ measure kümmel**

**1 measure lemon juice**

**dash Angostura bitters**

Stir with ice in a mixing jug, and strain into a small wineglass. Garnish with a half-slice of lemon.

## BROKEN LEG

**1 measure bourbon**

**2½ measures warmed apple juice (pressed type, not concentrate)**

Stir in a mug with a stick of cinnamon, and add a slice of lemon and a few raisins. One to cheer the spirits of one who has fallen foul of the nursery slopes.

## BOURBON FOG

This is a simple but effective punch recipe that requires equal quantities (say, a litre each for an enthusiastic bunch of summer revellers) of bourbon, cold strong black coffee and vanilla ice-cream.

On today's cocktail scene, whiskies have become quite as indispensable as vodka and tequila for creating thrilling mixtures.

## THE BOSS

**1½ measures bourbon**

**½ measure amaretto**

Pour the ingredients into a small tumbler half-filled with cracked ice. Throw in a cocktail cherry.

## SATISFACTION

**1 measure bourbon**

**½ measure Campari**

**½ measure sweet brown sherry**

**½ measure dark rum**

**lemonade to top up**

Add the ingredients in this order to a highball glass filled with broken ice, topping up with the lemonade. Add a half-slice of lemon. This drink was created for Sir Mick Jagger, in honour of one of the Rolling Stones' best-loved hits of the 1960s.

## GOLDMINE

**½ measure Scotch**

**½ measure Galliano**

**½ measure sweet brown sherry**

**1 tsp egg white**

**1 measure lime juice**

**1 measure lemonade**

Shake the first five ingredients well with ice, and strain into a tumbler containing a couple of ice-cubes. Add the lemonade. Decorate with a twist of orange peel and a cocktail cherry.

## WITCH HUNT

**1 measure Scotch**

**½ measure dry vermouth**

**¼ measure Strega**

**1 measure lemonade**

Add the ingredients in this order to a tumbler charged with plenty of cracked ice. Garnish with a half-slice of lemon. The name of the Italian liqueur in this cocktail, Strega, means 'witch'. At only a quarter of a measure's strength, you will literally be hunting its flavour as you drink it.

## ROYAL TURKEY

**1 measure Wild Turkey 101 bourbon**

**1 measure sloe gin**

**1 measure apricot brandy**

**2 measures pineapple juice**

**3 measures 7-UP**

Shake the first four ingredients with ice, and strain into a tall glass half-filled with broken ice. Add the 7-UP. Drink through straws. One of the increasing number of brand-specific cocktails.

## LARK

**1 measure Scotch**

**1 measure Grand Marnier**

**¼ measure grenadine**

**¼ measure lemon juice**

**sparkling orange drink (e.g. Fanta) to top up**

Add the ingredients in this order to a large wineglass over cracked ice, and top with fizzy orange. Decorate with entwined twists of orange and lemon.

## THE BAIRN

**2 measures Scotch**

**¾ measure Cointreau**

**1 tsp Campari**

Add the ingredients in this order to a small tumbler filled with cracked ice. Squeeze a bit of orange peel over the drink, and drop it in.

## WHISKY MELON SOUR

**1 measure Scotch or bourbon**

**1 measure Midori**

**1 measure lemon juice**

**1 tsp caster sugar**

Shake well with ice to dissolve the sugar, and strain into a tumbler. Add a half-slice of lemon. Many of today's formulas are souped-up versions of the classic recipes, with some exotic flavouring added. This one is very typical. It needs more lemon juice than a traditional Whisky Sour (qv), in order to counteract the syrupy sweetness of the melon liqueur, and still qualify on the tastebuds as a Sour.

## SOUL MANHATTAN

**2 measures Woodford Reserve bourbon**

**½ measure cherry brandy**

**1 tsp absinthe**

**1 tsp soft brown sugar**

Stir the bourbon and cherry brandy with ice in a tumbler. Sprinkle the sugar on to the peel side of a twist of orange, pour the absinthe over it and set it alight. Float this burning 'boat' on the surface of the drink. This was invented in 2003 by Michael Butt of London's Match Bars, and earned him first prize in a cocktail competition sponsored by the bourbon brand it contains.

## BROOKLYN

**1½ measures Canadian whisky**
**1 measure dry vermouth**
**dash maraschino**
**dash Amer Picon or white Dubonnet**

Shake with ice, and strain into a cocktail glass. Garnish with a twist of lemon.

## MAN O'WAR

**1 measure Wild Turkey 101 bourbon**
**1 measure orange curaçao**
**½ measure sweet red vermouth**
**½ measure lemon juice**

Shake with ice, and strain into a small tumbler half-filled with cracked ice. Add a twist of orange peel and a cocktail cherry.

## BLARNEY STONE

**2 measures Irish whiskey**

**1 tsp Cointreau**

**1 tsp Pernod**

**1 tsp maraschino**

**dash Angostura bitters**

Add to a small tumbler containing a couple of ice-cubes. Stir and garnish with a twist of orange.

# 5
# VODKA

It ought to be a surprise to find vodka so widely used as a cocktail base. After all, in most of its manifestations it is just a plain, simple, ultra-purified neutral spirit that may leave a smouldering burn in the throat, but actually tastes of fresh air. But then that is half its appeal.

Recent generations of younger drinkers have seized on vodka as their tipple precisely because it doesn't have the kind of assertively rich flavours that the darker spirits, such as brandy, dark rum and whisky, all possess. Even more than white rum or silver tequila, vodka insinuates itself in with whatever it is being mixed with, camouflaging itself like a chameleon.

Compared to those traditional dark spirits, it is a relative newcomer to Western drinking circles, having been around commercially for not much longer than tequila. When it was first sold in the West, by an American company that had obtained the formula from a Russian émigré named Smirnoff, it was viewed as the exotic hooch of communist eastern Europe, and as such, became something of a rebellious style accessory among disaffected American youth, at least until they discovered marijuana.

We should remember that vodka is by no means always a neutral spirit in its original countries of origin, Poland and Russia. There is a centuries-old tradition of flavoured vodkas, products often made in peasant households as a means of adding some supposedly health-giving properties to the staple liquor. Vodkas infused with herbs, spices, fruits and nuts are still widely made in eastern Europe, and increasingly in other countries too (Sweden's Absolut, with its citrus, pepper and blackcurrant versions, has been a fashionable brand in recent times).

In the recipes that follow, we have selected cocktails in which the vodka – flavoured or not – plays an integral role of its own in a drink, rather than those where it is simply added to a mixture to give an extra kick of alcohol.

## VODKA COLLINS

**2 measures vodka**
**juice of half a lemon**
**2 tsp caster sugar**
**soda water to top up**

Shake the first three ingredients with ice, and strain into a long glass containing a single cube of ice. Top with soda. The Collins was another of those simple nineteenth-century formulas (not a million miles away from the basic Fizz, as the eagle-eyed will note) that could be easily adapted to fit any base spirit. If a drink could be made with gin, as all such recipes could, then vodka, when it came along, was hardly going to upset the applecart.

## RUSSIAN COCKTAIL

**1 measure vodka**

**1 measure gin**

**1 measure white crème de cacao**

Shake with ice, and strain into a cocktail glass. This, one of Harry Craddock's earliest efforts with vodka for the *Savoy Cocktail Book* (1930), seems to speak of the exoticism with which the Russian spirit was first treated. Chocolate liqueur was a favoured partner for it in these early days, as will be seen again in the recipe below.

## BARBARA

**2 measures vodka**

**½ measure white crème de cacao**

**½ measure double cream**

Shake well with ice, and strain into a cocktail glass. Sprinkle grated chocolate on the surface.

## BLUE MONDAY

**1½ measures vodka**

**½ measure Cointreau**

**dash blue curaçao**

Shake with ice, and strain into a cocktail glass. In the 1920s, blue curaçao was not yet available, and so this drink was prepared with blue food colouring. Little did he know it, but Mr Craddock was fixing forever in the bartender's mind the association of blue drinks with vodka.

Perhaps the most famous of the old vodka cocktails is the Bloody Mary, invented at Harry's Bar in Paris shortly after the First World War by barman Ferdinand Petiot. Interestingly, this was originally conceived of primarily as a way of using not vodka but tomato juice, which was then a commercial novelty. Some accounts say the drink was named after a woman called Mary who was regularly stood up at the bar of Harry's, and used to nurse a few of these while waiting for a man who never showed up. Her amorous imprisonment reminded M. Petiot, so the story goes, of the incarceration of Mary, Queen of Scots, the original 'Bloody Mary'. Others simply say the drink was named after Mary Pickford, although another recipe had already been created in her honour, bearing her name (qv).

'To each his or her own' is the fashion with the Bloody Mary. The seasonings are very much a matter of individual taste, as is the garnish, but what must indispensably go into it is tomato juice, lemon juice, Worcestershire sauce and of course vodka. Such is the savoury satisfaction of the other components that the vodka completely disappears within the drink (it should never taste crudely alcoholic), and some even dispense with it altogether, in which case what you have is a Virgin Mary. We are not of this party, preferring the formula given opposite.

The Bloody Mary has two inimitably vital functions. It makes a fine aperitif, particularly at lunchtime, having a nourishing quality all its own, and – perhaps even more famously – it is a great restorer in the unfortunate and unforeseen event of a thundering hangover. The spiciness of the drink, and the fact that its hair-of-the-dog slug of alcohol is so efficiently disguised, will soon revive even the most ravaged of constitutions.

## BLOODY MARY

**2 measures vodka**

**1 tsp Worcestershire sauce**

**1 tsp lemon juice**

**4 dashes Tabasco**

**pinch celery seasoning**

**4 twists of the black pepper mill**

**tomato juice to top up**

Stir everything together in a mixing jug with ice, and strain into a tall glass half-filled with broken ice. Add a half-slice of lemon and, if desired, a stick of celery trimmed to just taller than the height of the glass.

Alternatively, the drink can be made in the glass. Put in the ice, and add the lemon juice and Worcestershire sauce, stirring to coat the lumps of ice. Add the other seasonings and the tomato juice, and stir it all up again. Finally, add the vodka and stir that well in too. Garnish with a half-slice of lemon.

## BULLSHOT

Proceed as for the Bloody Mary, but instead of topping the drink with tomato juice, use cold beef consommé from a can instead. If beef consommé doesn't present itself, try using one of those liquid fresh beef stocks from the supermarket chilled shelves.

## ALEXANDER THE GREAT

**1½ measures vodka**

**½ measure Kahlua**

**½ measure brown crème de cacao**

**½ measure double cream**

Shake well with ice, and strain into a cocktail glass. This variation on the Brandy Alexander (qv) was reportedly invented by the hugely successful singing star of 1930s Hollywood, Nelson Eddy.

## TSARINA

**1 measure vodka**

**¾ measure apricot brandy**

**½ measure dry vermouth**

**½ measure sweet red vermouth**

Shake with ice, and strain into a cocktail glass. Garnish with a twist of lemon. This is another of the many Russian-named early vodka cocktails. Below are a few more.

## TOVARICH

**1½ measures vodka**

**1 measure kümmel**

**juice of half a lime**

Shake with ice, and strain into a cocktail glass. Garnish with a slice of lime.

## BALLET RUSSE

**2 measures vodka**

**½ measure crème de cassis**

**1 tsp lime juice**

Shake with ice, and strain into a cocktail glass. Garnish with a slice of lime.

## BALALAIKA

**1½ measures vodka**

**¾ measure Cointreau**

**¾ measure lemon juice**

Shake with ice, and strain into a cocktail glass. Garnish with a twist of orange. This is a vodka version of the gin-based White Lady (qv).

## MOSCOW MULE

**2 measures vodka**

**¼ measure lime juice**

**ginger ale to top up**

Add the ingredients in this order to a tall glass half-filled with cracked ice. Add a slice of lime. This drink has certainly stood the test of time, to the extent that one of the leading vodka brands produces its own proprietary Moscow Mule in 330ml bottles. The recipe was originally just vodka and ginger ale, but the lime undeniably gives it pep.

## VODKA MARTINI/VODKATINI

**2 measures vodka**

**½ measure dry vermouth**

Stir with ice in a mixing jug, and strain into a cocktail glass. Add a stuffed olive, if required, or a twist of lemon, if preferred. As many of the old gin cocktails were tried out with vodka once it became widely available in the USA in the 1940s, the vodka martini was a cinch. It was the version favoured by everyone from the novelist Dashiel Hammett to international espionage ace James Bond, although he famously prefers his 'shaken, not stirred'.

## DEVIL'S TORCH

**1½ measures vodka**

**1 measure dry vermouth**

**½ tsp grenadine**

Shake with ice, and strain into a cocktail glass. Garnish with a twist of lemon. This recipe comes from a British cocktail book of 1937, and is little more than a pink Vodka Martini.

## BUZZ-BOMB

**1 measure vodka**

**1 measure Bénédictine**

**1 measure cognac**

**1 measure Cointreau**

**1 measure lime juice**

**champagne to top up**

Shake the first five ingredients with ice, and strain into a tall narrow glass filled up with cracked ice. Top with champagne ('a fill-up of the best vintage champagne', in the recipe given in Lucius Beebe's *Stork Club Bar Book* of 1946). A somewhat ostentatious drink for a minor celebration. By the end of the glass, you will have quite forgotten what it was you were celebrating.

## SCREWDRIVER

**2 measures vodka**
**½ tsp caster sugar**
**freshly squeezed orange juice to top up**

Ice a tall glass, add the vodka and sugar and stir to dissolve the latter. Top up with orange juice, and add a twist of orange peel. The forerunner of all the vodka-and-oranges downed in bars and nightclubs ever since, the Screwdriver supposedly derived its name from an American oil rig worker of the 1950s who, finding himself short of a bar spoon, used the nearest implement to hand to stir the drink. If juice from a carton is used instead, use the pressed type, not concentrate, but don't bother with the pinch of sugar.

## GIPSY

**2 measures vodka**
**1 measure Bénédictine**
**dash Angostura bitters**

Shake with ice, and strain into a cocktail glass. Garnish with a half-slice of lemon.

## BLACK RUSSIAN

**1 measure vodka**

**1 measure Kahlua or Tia Maria**

Serve on the rocks in a small tumbler. This is the 1950s original of what became one of the most popular cocktails of the 1970s and '80s. What elevated it to the level of a craze in the later era was the practice of serving it in a long glass and topping it up with Coca-Cola. For those who like cola, this is an irresistibly luxurious drink. For mature adults, the original is a much more sophisticated mixture.

The cola brigade helped to spawn many variations, though, among which were the following:

## WHITE RUSSIAN

**1 measure vodka**

**1 measure Kahlua or Tia Maria**

**1 measure double cream**

Shake well with ice, and strain into a cocktail glass. In some manifestations, the White Russian is made by mixing the alcoholic ingredients with ice in a tumbler, and then pouring the cream on top as a float.

## RED RUSSIAN

**1 measure vodka**

**½ measure cherry brandy**

**½ measure apricot brandy**

Shake with ice, and pour without straining into a small tumbler. This variation was invented in Iceland in 1969.

## HARVEY WALLBANGER

**2 measures vodka**

**4 measures orange juice**

**½ measure Galliano**

Pour the vodka and orange juice into a generously iced glass. Float the Galliano carefully on the surface. This was a much-loved 1970s formula. A story is told of a San Francisco surfboarder called Harvey who liked a slug of the spicy Italian liqueur it contains in his Screwdriver. After downing several of them on one occasion, he was seen to be walking into walls, for which piece of drollery this recipe was named after him. The drink is best made with pressed orange juice from a carton, which has a thicker texture than the freshly squeezed article, and therefore helps the liqueur to float.

## SLOW COMFORTABLE SCREW AGAINST THE WALL

**1 measure vodka**

**¾ measure sloe gin**

**¾ measure Southern Comfort**

**orange juice to top up**

**½ measure Galliano**

Shake the first three ingredients with ice, and strain into a highball glass half-filled with cracked ice. Top with cartoned orange juice, and garnish with a half-slice of orange. Float the Galliano on top. The slightly desperate name of this drink derives of course from its various ingredients, with the Galliano adding the gratuitous wall detail (as in 'Wallbanger').

## BLUE LAGOON

**1 measure vodka**

**1 measure blue curaçao**

**lemonade to top up**

Add the ingredients in this order to a tall glass half-filled with broken ice. Garnish with a half-slice of lemon and a cocktail cherry. This drink was originally created in the early 1960s at Harry's Bar in Paris, when it was a short drink made with equal measures of vodka, blue curaçao and lemon juice. The recipe above became popular in the 1970s, and remains the definitive version today.

## KATINKA

**1½ measures vodka**

**1 measure apricot brandy**

**½ measure lime juice**

Shake with ice, and strain into a cocktail glass filled with crushed ice. Garnish with a twist of lime.

## APRÈS SKI

**1 measure vodka**

**1 measure green crème de menthe**

**1 measure Pernod**

**lemonade to top up**

Shake the first three ingredients with ice, and strain into a highball glass. Top with lemonade, and add a half-slice of lemon and a couple of mint leaves. The flavours in this drink – aniseed, mint and lemon – are very pronounced, even slightly discordant, and you will still be tasting it about half-an-hour after you've finished one. It isn't therefore a suitable aperitif, but as a dash of mid-afternoon jollity (after a spin on the piste, its name seems to suggest), it is certainly an experience.

## GOLDEN TANG

**2 measures vodka**

**1 measure Strega**

**½ measure crème de banane**

**½ measure orange juice**

Shake with ice, and strain into a wineglass filled with crushed ice. Garnish with a twist of lemon. The formula in Michael Walker's cocktail book of 1980 uses double these measures in a single drink, and attributes the recipe to some mysterious tour guide, who used it as a cure for gastric turmoil in foreign climes.

## DEB'S DELIGHT

**1 measure vodka**

**1 measure apricot brandy**

**½ measure anisette**

**pouring cream to top up**

Stir the first three ingredients with ice in a mixing glass until cold, and strain into a small tumbler charged with broken ice. Top with thin cream. This should encourage even the shyest of débutantes in her coming-out.

## SALTY DOG

**2 measures vodka**

**grapefruit juice to top up**

Frost the rim of a highball glass by dipping it first in grapefruit juice and then in salt. Half-fill it with cracked ice, add the vodka and then top with grapefruit juice. Decorate with a twist of grapefruit peel. The combined saltiness and sourness of this drink will prove most appetising.

Many of the most popular drinks today derive their appeal from mixtures of non-alcoholic ingredients on a simple, unassertive spirit base. Of these, the Sea Breeze – actually a 1960s recipe – is absolutely characteristic.

## SEA BREEZE

**2 measures vodka**

**3 measures grapefruit juice**

**2 measures cranberry juice**

Add the ingredients in this order to a generously iced highball glass. Throw in a wedge of lime.

## COSMOPOLITAN

**1½ measures citron vodka**

**½ measure Cointreau**

**¼ measure lime juice**

**1 measure cranberry juice**

Shake with ice, and strain into a cocktail glass. Squeeze a piece of orange peel over the surface of the drink so that its oil sprays out. The Cosmopolitan is one of the most requested drinks in today's bar repertoire. This recipe, given by Dale Degroff in *The Craft of the Cocktail* (2002), was formulated by him in the 1990s, and has found favour with, amongst others, Madonna.

## JAPANESE SLIPPER

**1½ measures vodka**

**1½ measures Midori**

**¾ measure lemon juice**

Shake with ice, and strain into a wineglass or champagne saucer. Garnish with a half-slice of lemon and a cube of canteloupe melon on a cocktail stick.

## PINK CORAL

**1 measure vodka**

**½ measure Passoa**

**2 measures pineapple juice**

**1 measure passion-fruit juice**

**1 measure guava juice**

**½ measure grenadine**

**dash Angostura bitters**

Shake with ice, and strain into a large wineglass. Garnish with slices of pineapple and guava.

## CHERRY BOMB

**1 measure cherry vodka**

**½ measure pale dry sherry**

**½ measure tequila**

**½ measure Grand Marnier**

**cherry cola to top up**

Add the ingredients in this order to a highball glass half-filled with cracked ice. Garnish with a cocktail cherry on a stick.

## THANK HEAVEN FOR SMALL NURSES

**1 measure limonnaya**

**½ measure Drambuie**

**¼ measure Bénédictine**

**2 measures mandarin juice (from a can of segments in unsweetened juice)**

Shake with ice, and strain into a tumbler with a couple of ice-cubes in it. Garnish with a mandarin segment on a stick. We are at a loss to explain the name of this drink, which appears in Robert Cross's book of 1996, *The Classic 1000 Cocktails.*

## RECOVERER

**1 measure limonnaya**

**1 measure peach schnapps**

**2 measures mandarin juice (as in the above recipe)**

**1 tsp grenadine**

Shake with ice, and strain into a small tumbler. Garnish with a mandarin segment.

## COOCH BEHAR

**2 measures pieprzówka**

**4 measures tomato juice**

Add to a rocks glass containing plenty of cracked ice. Garnish with a half-slice of lemon. A Bloody Mary for corner-cutters, this drink is said to have been invented by the Maharajah of Cooch Behar (or Koch Bihar), India.

Coffee-based cocktails became all the rage in the 1990s. The first of these was created by the legendary London master, Dick Bradsell, for the Match Bar chain, while the credit for the second must go to the Exhibit Bar in Balham, south London.

## VODKA ESPRESSO

**1 measure vodka**

**1 measure Kahlua**

**1½ measures freshly made strong espresso coffee**

Shake with ice until the coffee has cooled, and strain into a cocktail glass. Garnish with three coffee beans.

## SHAMROCK ESPRESSO

**1 measure Absolut vodka**

**1 measure Bailey's Irish Cream**

**1 measure butterscotch schnapps**

**1 measure espresso** (as above)

Shake with ice, and strain into a goblet-style cocktail glass half-filled with crushed ice.

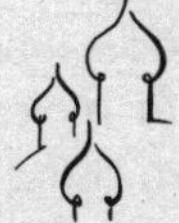

# 6

# RUM

Among the half-dozen basic spirits (rum, gin, brandy, whisky, vodka and tequila), rum all too often appears to be the poor relation, not in terms of quality but of popularity. White rum, led by the international brand leader Bacardi, lacks for nothing in terms of sales volumes, of course, but the coloured rums – golden and dark – are frequently overlooked. Some say they don't know what to mix it with, a dilemma we hope the following pages will swiftly resolve.

Born ignobly of the slave trade, when it played a crucial part in the transatlantic shipments of molasses, raw spirit and captive Africans, rum has always been associated with maritime endeavour. Until 1970, it was issued as a perk of the job to able-bodied seamen in Britain's Royal Navy, and must have contributed in a fair few instances to making them a little less able-bodied than they had been.

Rum is a product of the distillation of sugar cane, and is a particular speciality of certain of the Caribbean islands and of the northern nations of South America, such as Guyana. The products of these often tiny distilleries are worth seeking out in specialist suppliers, airport shops and while on holiday in the region, since they are always much more complex (and occasionally more powerful) spirits than the big-name brands.

As well as the three basic styles of commercial rum – white, dark and golden, the last of which is a medium style sometimes known as 'light' – there is also naval-strength rum, which can be up to 57% alcohol, and a high-grade product bottled at what is known as 'overproof' – in excess of 57%. Another style beginning to attract attention in recent years is spiced rum. These rums have had a bouquet of aromatic spices infused in them, lending them fugitive scents and flavours of ginger, chilli and vanilla.

## RUM PUNCH (I)

**1½ measures dark rum**

**1 measure brandy**

**½ measure lemon juice**

**3 measures hot water**

**1 tsp caster sugar**

Add the ingredients to a tall glass with a spoon standing in it to conduct the heat of the water. Give the drink a thorough stirring to dissolve the sugar, and add a half-slice of lemon. Variations on this nineteenth-century recipe, from California viticulturist George A Saintsbury's *Notes from a Cellar Book*, have proliferated over the years, but Mr Saintsbury stated of this one, 'I never knew this mixture found fault with by respectable persons of any age, sex or condition, from undergraduates to old ladies, at any hour between sunset and sunrise.'

## RUM PUNCH (II)

By the early years of the twentieth century, Rum Punch was more familiarly a cold drink, as in this fairly racy formula from a book called *Cocktails: How To Mix Them*, by Robert Vermeire, who had seen service at the American Bar of the Casino Municipal in Nice, and also at the Embassy Club in London.

**3 measures dark rum**
**juice of half a lemon**
**1 tbsp sugar syrup**
**soda water to top up**

Shake the first three ingredients with ice, and strain into a tall glass packed with cracked ice and a slice of lemon. Top with soda.

Another concoction from the 1800s was the Daisy, essentially a soured spirit with a touch of either syrup, such as grenadine, or a sweet liqueur like maraschino, served as a long drink topped with sparkling water.

## RUM DAISY

**2 measures dark rum**
**juice of half a lemon**
**1 tsp maraschino**
**1 tsp sugar syrup**
**soda water to top up**

Shake the first four ingredients with ice, and strain into a highball glass. Top with soda, and add a half-slice of lemon.

The Flip dates back even further, to the closing stages of the eighteenth century, when over-indulgence in it was sternly counselled against in a treatise against immoderate drinking by Dr Benjamin Rush, one of the founding fathers of modern American medicine. It's an egg drink, which we might consider a rather effete mixture nowadays, although it was then one of the preferred tipples of American sailors. Be sure your eggs are very fresh and free-range before embarking on it.

## RUM FLIP

**3 measures dark rum**

**1½ tsps caster sugar**

**1 egg**

Shake all the ingredients very briskly with ice to amalgamate the egg, and strain into a tumbler. Sprinkle the top with ground nutmeg. A little of the syrup from a jar of crystallised ginger can be added for that extra touch of spice. The Flip could essentially be made with any alcohol base, including brandy, whisky, sweet brown sherry or tawny port.

## BACARDI SPECIAL

**1½ measures Bacardi white rum**

**1 measure gin**

**1 tsp grenadine**

**juice of half a lime**

Shake with ice, and strain into a cocktail glass. This is the souped-up version of the original Bacardi cocktail, which didn't contain the gin. Whether you choose to use it or not, the white rum chosen must be the Bacardi brand.

## DAIQUIRI

**2 measures white rum**

**juice of a quarter of a lemon (or half a lime)**

**1 tsp caster sugar**

Shake well with ice, and strain into a cocktail glass. This is the original Daiquiri, first formulated in the 1890s and named after a town in Cuba. It wasn't long before the Daiquiri started being jollied up with all kinds of fruit flavours (see below), but it was quite jolly enough as it was, thank you, being a short, razor-sharp cocktail of bracing piquancy. It is, of course, nothing other than a white rum sour.

## FROZEN FRUIT DAIQUIRI (Strawberry Version)

**2 measures white rum**

**½ measure maraschino**

**6 medium-sized strawberries**

**2 measures sugar syrup**

**juice of half a lime**

Add the ingredients to an electric blender with plenty of crushed ice, and whizz until the strawberries have been completely puréed. Pour into a goblet-type wineglass, and garnish with a whole small strawberry on a cocktail stick. Other successful Frozen Daiquiris can be made with very ripe peeled peach or with banana. The appropriately flavoured liqueur can be substituted in all these recipes for the maraschino.

## TOM & JERRY

This drink was created by the grandaddy of all cocktail bartenders, Jerry Thomas, in the 1850s in St Louis, Missouri. It was a seasonal drink intended to be served at the first cold snap of winter. As it is based on an egg batter, it is more efficient to make it in quantity. This recipe should comfortably do four.

*For the batter:*
**3 eggs**
**3 tbsps caster sugar**
**1 measure dark rum**
**pinch bicarbonate of soda**
**pinch powdered cinnamon**
**pinch allspice**
**pinch ground cloves**

Separate the eggs, and whisk the whites until they are stiff enough not to budge when the bowl is turned upside down. Add a third of the sugar with the bicarbonate, which will prevent the sugar from sinking in the mixture. Beat the yolks with the rum, spices and the remaining sugar, then fold the beaten egg-white into it, using a metal spoon.

*For each drink:*
**1 measure dark rum**
**1 measure brandy**
**steamed milk for topping up**

To prepare each drink, put about a tablespoon of the batter into a coffee glass (the kind with a handle used for serving caffe latte). Add the rum and brandy, and top with hot milk. Sprinkle with ground nutmeg. As will be appreciated, this is one of the most labour-intensive cocktails in this book, but as your guests are welcomed in from the cold on a November or December night, you will find them mighty glad of it.

## MOJITO

**2 measures golden rum**
**1 tsp caster sugar**
**juice of half a lime**
**soda water to top up**

Add the first three ingredients to a highball glass with a couple of cubes of ice, and stir to dissolve the sugar. Top with soda. This is an old Cuban recipe, sometimes enhanced by the addition of a sprig of crushed mint.

## PLANTER'S PUNCH

**2 measures golden rum**
**2 measures fresh orange juice**
**1 measure lemon juice**
**1 measure pineapple juice**

Shake with ice, and strain into a tumbler, liberally garnished with fresh fruit. The original Planter's Punch was barely more than a rum and orange with a dash of lemon in it, but it soon acquired a host of other fruit flavours. Some add a dash of Angostura too, but essentially the rum should be the only alcohol in the drink.

## BETWEEN THE SHEETS

**1 measure white rum**
**1 measure brandy**
**1 measure Cointreau**
**dash lemon juice**

Shake with ice, and strain into a cocktail glass laden with crushed ice. Some recipes don't bother with the dash of lemon, leaving the drink entirely composed of strong alcohol, while others stir it in a jug rather than shaking it. It is as well to leave some ice in it, however you fancy it, as this is a lethally powerful mixture.

## MARY PICKFORD

**1½ measures white rum**

**1½ measures pineapple juice**

**1 tsp grenadine**

**dash maraschino**

Shake with ice, and strain into a cocktail glass filled with crushed ice. Add a cocktail cherry on a stick. This drink, created in honour of the star of films such as *Pollyanna* (1920) and one of the founders of United Artists, was invented in Havana in the 1920s, when the United States was in the grip of Prohibition.

## PARISIAN BLONDE

**1 measure dark rum**

**1 measure orange curaçao**

**1 measure sweetened double cream**

Shake well with ice, and strain into a cocktail glass. A little more bitter than today's cream cocktails, this is nonetheless a good mixture that remained popular well into the postwar period.

## PALMETTO

**1½ measures dark rum**

**1½ measures sweet red vermouth**

**2 dashes orange bitters (or curaçao)**

Shake with ice, and strain into a cocktail glass. Garnish with a cocktail cherry.

## MILLIONAIRE

**1 measure dark rum**

**1 measure apricot brandy**

**1 measure sloe gin**

**juice of a lime**

**dash grenadine**

Shake with ice, and strain into a cocktail glass. Add a slice of lime. There were many drinks with this name around in the 1920s. Other versions were based on gin or bourbon, but this is about the most exotic in taste.

## PRESIDENTE

**2 measures white rum, Cuban if possible**

**1 measure orange curaçao**

**1 tsp grenadine**

Stir the ingredients with ice in a mixing jug, and strain into a small tumbler. Later versions of this drink were made distinctly drier by the addition of half a measure of dry vermouth. It was named in honour of an old military dictator of Cuba, when such people were thought worth honouring.

## KNICKERBOCKER SPECIAL

**½ measure orange curaçao**

**2 measures dark rum**

**1 tsp crème de framboise**

**1 tsp fresh orange juice**

**1 tsp lemon juice**

Shake with ice, and strain into a cocktail glass or small wine goblet. Add a pineapple chunk. This drink is intended to mimic the fruity ice-cream dessert of (nearly) the same name.

## CHINESE COCKTAIL

**2 measures dark rum**

**1 measure grenadine**

**¼ measure orange curaçao**

**¼ measure maraschino**

**dash Angostura bitters**

Shake with ice, and strain into a cocktail glass. Add a cherry on a stick. The relatively high proportion of grenadine makes this a rather syrupy cocktail, but one that is absolutely typical of its 1920s era. What makes it Chinese, we hesitate to guess.

Sticking with the same theme, we next present:

## SHANGHAI

**1 measure dark rum**

**¾ measure lemon juice**

**¼ measure anisette (or Pernod)**

**2 dashes grenadine**

Shake with ice, and strain into a cocktail glass. Garnish with a half-slice of lemon.

## LITTLE DEVIL

**1 measure white rum**

**1 measure gin**

**½ measure Cointreau**

**½ measure lemon juice**

Shake with ice, and strain into a cocktail glass. Add a half-slice of lemon.

## DUNLOP

**2 measures dark rum**

**1 measure pale dry sherry**

**dash Angostura bitters**

Stir the ingredients well with ice, and strain into a tumbler. An extremely dry and bitter cocktail for very sophisticated palates.

## BVD

**1 measure Bacardi white rum**

**1 measure dry vermouth**

**1 measure dry gin**

Shake with ice, and strain into a cocktail glass. Do not garnish. Another extremely dry (and powerful) one, this derives its name, obliquely enough, from the initials of its ingredients – Bacardi, Vermouth and Dry gin. The pallidly risqué joke was that 'BVDs' was also a generic name for a type of men's underwear, named after the original manufacturers, Bradley, Voorhes and Day.

## MARAGATO

**1 measure white rum**

**1 measure dry vermouth**

**1 measure sweet red vermouth**

**dash kirsch**

**juice of half a lemon**

**juice of one-third of a lime**

**1 tsp caster sugar**

Shake with ice, and strain into a wineglass. Garnish with half-slices of lemon and lime. There is a recipe for a Spanish stew containing blood pudding that has the same name. The cocktail was created at the Floridita Bar in Havana in the twenties.

## SONORA

**1½ measures white rum**

**1½ measures calvados (or applejack)**

**2 dashes apricot brandy**

**1 dash lemon juice**

Shake with ice, and strain into a cocktail glass. Garnish with an unpeeled slice of apple.

## FULL HOUSE

**1½ measures white rum**

**¾ measure Swedish punch**

**¾ measure dry vermouth**

Shake with ice, and strain into a cocktail glass. Do not garnish.

## CUBA LIBRE

**2 measures dark rum**

**juice of a quarter of a lime**

**Coca-Cola to top up**

Put the rum and lime in a tall glass, and top with Coke. Throw in a wedge of lime. This, the best-known of all Cuban cocktails, was invented very soon after Coca-Cola began to be marketed in the late nineteenth century.

## MAI TAI

**2 measures dark rum**

**1 measure orange curaçao**

**1 measure lime juice**

**½ measure orgeat syrup (or amaretto)**

Shake with ice, and strain into a freshly iced tumbler. Decorate with a wedge of lime and a couple of mint leaves. This drink, much re-invented since its creation, now often has a measure of grenadine poured slowly into it, so that it forms a blood-red layer at the bottom of the drink.

## ANN SHERIDAN

**2 measures Bacardi white rum**

**1 measure orange curaçao**

**juice of half a lime**

Shake with ice, and strain into a tumbler. Drop the shell of the lime into the drink. Cocktails named after film stars have been a constant since the days of the silent screen. This one was created by New York barman Harry Kaye in the 1940s.

## FBI FIZZ

**½ measure dark rum**

**½ measure bourbon**

**½ measure cherry brandy**

**soda water to top up**

Shake the first three ingredients with ice, and strain into a highball glass with a couple of ice cubes in it. Top with soda, and add a twist of orange peel.

## OLYMPIA

**1½ measures dark rum**

**1 measure cherry brandy**

**juice of half a lime**

Shake with ice, and strain into a cocktail glass. Decorate with a slice of lime and a cherry. Not to be confused with Olympic, a brandy cocktail (qv).

## SCHNORKEL

**2 measures golden rum**

**½ measure Pernod**

**juice of a lime**

**1 tsp caster sugar**

Shake well with ice, and strain into a cocktail glass. This drink was named after a wartime submarine.

## RUM BANA

**3 measures dark rum**

**1 measure lemon juice**

**1 tsp caster sugar**

**1 ripe peeled banana**

Blend with crushed ice in a liquidiser, and serve in a goblet-style cocktail glass. A strong, and wholly irresistible mixture from the early days of electric mixers.

## BROOKLYNITE

**2 measures dark rum**

**½ measure clear honey**

**dash lime juice**

**dash Angostura bitters**

Shake well with ice, and strain into a cocktail glass. Garnish with a slice of lime.

## DEVIL'S TAIL

**1½ measures overproof rum**

**1½ measures vodka**

**½ measure lime juice**

**1 measure grenadine**

**apricot brandy to float**

Blend the first four ingredients with crushed ice in a liquidiser, and strain into a wineglass. Float a teaspoon or so of apricot brandy on top. Only the very intrepid or the very foolish would attempt to negotiate this forties cocktail.

## ZOMBIE

**1 measure golden rum**

**½ measure dark rum**

**½ measure white rum**

**1 measure orange curaçao**

**¼ measure absinthe**

**1 measure lemon juice**

**1 measure pineapple juice**

**1 measure orange juice**

**¼ measure grenadine**

**1 tsp overproof rum**

Blend all but the last ingredient with smashed ice in a liquidiser, and strain into a highball glass. Sprinkle the teaspoon of overproof rum on the surface of the drink. Garnish with slices of pineapple, orange, lime and a sprig of mint. This is a surefire route to damnation and, although it became prominent in the 1980s, it has in fact been around since the thirties, when it was invented – in something like this form – at a Hollywood restaurant called Don the Beachcomber. There are many variations on this recipe, but it always involves plenty of rum, one or two liqueurs and at least three kinds of fruit juice. Its name indicates the state to which it will reduce the drinker if taken in quantity.

## DOROTHY LAMOUR

**1 measure light rum**

**1 measure crème de banane**

**½ measure mango juice**

**½ measure lime juice**

Shake with ice, and strain into a cocktail glass. Garnish with a cube of ripe mango. Another film star tribute, this one honours Bing Crosby and Bob Hope's co-star in the series of *Road* movies that began with *The Road to Singapore* (1940).

## PIÑA COLADA

**2 measures white rum**

**2 measures pineapple juice**

**1½ measures coconut cream**

**1 tsp caster sugar**

Blend the ingredients with shaved ice in a liquidiser, and strain into a bowl-shaped cocktail glass. Garnish with a slice of pineapple and a cherry. This was one of the most popular cocktails of the 1980s revival, brought back to cooler climes by holidaymakers in the Caribbean. It should authentically be served in a hollowed-out pineapple shell, in which case the flesh of the fruit can be liquidised and strained, and some of it used to provide the juice in the recipe. One or two recipes, going down a more savoury route, opt to add a couple of dashes of Angostura bitters and even a pinch of salt to it, but we suspect the formula above is roughly the one everybody remembers and loves.

## SCORPION

**2 measures golden rum**
**½ measure brandy**
**1 measure orange juice**
**1 measure lemon juice**
**¼ measure orgeat syrup (or amaretto)**

Shake with ice, and strain into a tumbler with some cracked ice in it. Add a half-slice of orange.

## GOLDEN GATE

**1 measure dark rum**
**½ measure gin**
**¼ measure brown crème de cacao**
**¼ measure lemon juice**
**pinch of ground ginger**

Shake with ice, and strain into a cocktail glass. Garnish with a half-slice of lemon.

## APRICOT LADY

**1 measure golden rum**

**1 measure apricot brandy**

**¼ measure orange curaçao**

**½ measure lime juice**

**white of half an egg**

Blend with crushed ice in a liquidiser, and strain into a cocktail glass. Garnish with a slice of ripe apricot, and serve with straws.

## SAN JUAN

**2 measures golden rum**

**1½ measures grapefruit juice**

**¼ measure lime juice**

**¼ measure coconut milk**

**1 tsp cognac to float**

Shake the first four ingredients with ice, and strain into a champagne saucer. Float the brandy on the surface. Decorate with a twist of grapefruit.

## LEEWARD

**1 measure golden rum**

**½ measure calvados**

**½ measure sweet red vermouth**

Shake with ice, and strain into a tumbler with a couple of ice-cubes in it. Add a half-slice of lemon.

## SUNSET IN PARADISE

**1 measure dark rum**

**¼ measure Cointreau**

**¼ measure sweet red vermouth**

**½ measure lime juice**

**1 tsp demerara sugar**

Blend with crushed ice in a liquidiser, and strain into a cocktail glass. Garnish with a twist of orange peel and a cherry. This is a highly attractive 1980s recipe from transatlantic bartender Michael Walker.

## LARCHMONT

**2 measures white rum**

**1 measure Grand Marnier**

**½ measure lime juice**

Shake with ice, and strain into a small tumbler half-filled with crushed ice. Add a slice of lime.

## PETITE FLEUR

**1 measure white rum**

**1 measure Cointreau**

**1 measure pink grapefruit juice**

Shake with ice, and strain into a cocktail glass. Decorate with a twist of orange. The 'Little Flower' is a perfectly balanced and hugely refreshing cocktail.

## JULIA

**1 measure white rum**

**1 measure amaretto**

**1 measure double cream**

**6 ripe strawberries**

Blend with crushed ice in a liquidiser, and strain into a wineglass. Garnish with a whole strawberry on a stick. A 1970s American recipe that makes a wonderful summer party starter.

## BLUE HAWAIIAN

**1½ measures white rum**

**½ measure dark rum**

**½ measure blue curaçao**

**3 measures pineapple juice**

**1 measure coconut cream**

Blend with crushed ice in a liquidiser, and strain into a highball glass. Decorate with a chunk of pineapple and a cocktail cherry. As will be readily noted by the percipient, this is a stronger, bluer, updated version of the Piña Colada.

## ESCAPE ROUTE

**1 measure golden rum**

**1 measure Punt e Mes (or red Dubonnet)**

**½ measure crème de fraise**

**lemonade to top up**

Half-fill a tall glass with cracked ice. Add the ingredients in the order above, and throw in a whole small strawberry.

## WHITE BAT

**2 measures white rum**

**¾ measure Kahlua**

**2 measures single cream**

**cola to top up**

Add the first three ingredients to a tall glass filled with broken ice. Stir, then top with cola. Drink through a straw. This is a Dale Degroff recipe of enormous appeal, a superior variation on what used to be known as the White Russian.

## CAFÉ TRINIDAD

**1 measure dark rum**

**¾ measure Tia Maria**

**¾ measure amaretto**

**1 measure double cream**

Shake well with ice, and strain into a goblet-type wineglass. Dust the surface with ground nutmeg.

## PLATINUM BLONDE

**1 measure golden rum**

**1 measure Grand Marnier**

**1 measure double cream**

Shake well with ice, and strain into a cocktail glass. Decorate with a twist of mandarin orange peel. Another creamy, dreamy cocktail, bringing about a superb marriage of rum and orange brandy flavours.

## EMERALD STAR

**1 measure white rum**

**1 measure Midori**

**½ measure apricot brandy**

**½ measure lime juice**

**1 measure passion-fruit juice**

Shake with ice, and strain into a large goblet. Add a slice of lime.

## SAN SALVADOR

**1½ measures dark rum**

**1 measure orange curaçao**

**½ measure lime juice**

**2 measures fresh orange juice**

Shake with ice, and strain into a tumbler on the rocks. Add twists of orange and lime peel.

## SAILING BY

**1 measure white rum**

**1 measure crème de myrtille**

**½ measure ruby port**

**¼ measure lemon juice**

**2 measures ginger ale**

Shake the first four ingredients with ice, and strain into a large wineglass. Add the ginger ale, and garnish with a half-slice of lemon. A riot of complementary flavours distinguishes this recipe, from cocktail author Robert Cross.

## RUM RUNNER

**1 measure dark rum**

**1 measure crème de mûre**

**1 measure crème de banane**

**½ measure white rum**

**½ measure pineapple juice**

**½ measure grenadine**

**½ measure lemon juice**

**1 tsp orgeat syrup (or amaretto)**

Blend with crushed ice in a liquidiser, and strain into a large goblet. Decorate with a pineapple cube and a cocktail cherry.

## LOVE IN THE AFTERNOON

**2 measures dark rum**

**½ measure crème de fraise**

**1 measure fresh orange juice**

**¾ measure coconut cream**

**½ measure sugar syrup**

**½ measure double cream**

**4 strawberries**

Blend with crushed ice in a liquidiser, and strain into a large wineglass. Garnish with a thinly sliced strawberry on a cocktail stick, and serve with two thick straws. An aphrodisiac formula, if ever there was.

## ANGEL'S TREAT

**1½ measures dark rum**
**1 measure amaretto**
**1½ measures whipping cream**
**½ tsp sieved cocoa powder**

Shake well with ice, and strain into a cocktail glass. Sprinkle the drink with grated dark chocolate. Robert Cross says this is 'one for the chocoholics'.

Mr Benson, whose business interests find him frequently in the Maldives, has introduced this cocktail to the region, where it has been received with great plaudits. It makes a fine aperitif.

## JEFFREY'S COCKTAIL

**2 measures Pusser's dark rum**
**juice of half a lime**
**soda water to top up**

Add the first two ingredients to a tumbler half-filled with mineral water ice-cubes. Stir, and then add soda to taste, according to whether a shorter or longer drink is required. Garnish with a slice of lime.

Mr Walton, whose business interests take him frequently to his computer terminal in the corner of the room, offers the following complementary digestif.

## STUART'S COCKTAIL

**1 measure golden rum**

**¾ measure crème de framboise**

**¼ measure absinthe**

**½ measure lemon juice**

Shake with ice, and strain into a cocktail glass. Garnish with a raspberry and a half-slice of lemon.

# 7

# TEQUILA

Mexico's claim to spirit fame, tequila, deserves its place among the world's classic drinks. It is a product of singular distinction and the only one made from cactus. In fact, the agave plant that the spirit is derived from is not technically a cactus at all, but a huge, ugly, spiky member of the lily family, but cactus hooch is, we suspect, how tequila will always be viewed.

Starting life as a light, fermented 'beer' called *pulque*, it is distilled twice like Scotch in copper stills, and comes in three age categories. Silver (or blanco) tequila is the freshly made product, diluted to bottling strength (usually around 37.5%), and not given any ageing.

Spirits that have been given a brief period of resting in wood (perhaps a couple of months) are labelled 'reposado', while those that have been cask-aged long enough to have taken up some colour from the wood – i.e. at least a year – are known as 'añejo'. Gold (or 'oro') tequila may appear the same colour as those aged tequilas, but has merely been coloured with caramel to look the part.

When tequila was first introduced into the North American and European markets, nobody quite knew what to do with it. There was the famous 'shooting' ritual, in which one licked a pinch of salt off the back of one's hand, swigged down a shot of neat tequila, and then bit into a wedge of lime. This progression of flavours has a certain sour, savoury appeal to it, but the actual ritual is, quite frankly, something of a bore after about three rounds of it. The more fashionable practice since the 1980s has been tequila-slamming (for which procedure, see page 133).

Tequila is acquiring new cocktail recipes for itself all the time. We hope the following pages will encourage you to experiment further.

## MARGARITA

**1½ measures silver tequila**
**1 measure triple sec (or Cointreau)**
**¾ measure lime juice**

Prepare a chilled cocktail glass by moistening the rim with lime juice, and dipping it in salt. Shake the ingredients with ice, and strain into the glass. Garnish with a slender wedge of lime. This, the most famous tequila cocktail of them all, appears to have originated in 1948 in a restaurant in Tijuana, Mexico. It was created by the proprietor, one Danny Herrera, for the actress Marjorie Cole, who found that tequila was the only spirit that didn't disagree with her. 'Margarita' was the nearest Hispanic equivalent to her name. Some people substitute lemon juice for the lime, which gives an almost equal amount of bite to the final result, but doesn't taste quite as Mexican.

## FROZEN MARGARITA

The widely loved Frozen Margarita is more or less the same recipe, but the drink is made in an electric blender with a fistful of broken ice, and poured without straining. Alternatively, some shake the cocktail in the normal way, but then strain into a cocktail glass that is filled to the brim with crushed ice. The triple sec in the recipe can then be replaced with almost any other liqueur for your Frozen Margarita variations. (See below for a couple of the most successful.)

## TEQUILA SUNRISE

**2 measures silver tequila**

**orange juice to top up (non-concentrate juice from a carton, rather than freshly squeezed)**

**1 dsp grenadine**

Half-fill a highball glass with cracked ice, and add the tequila and orange juice. Pour the grenadine carefully on to the surface of the drink, so that it sinks slowly through, thus creating the famous 'sunrise' effect. Although it was all the rage in the 1970s, this cocktail was invented back in the 1940s. Despite its rather tricksy presentation, it is a very harmonious blend of flavours.

## PARKEROO

**1 measure silver tequila**

**2 measures pale dry sherry**

Pour the two ingredients over crushed ice, allow the drink to chill and dilute, and then transfer it into a saucer-style champagne glass. Invented at New York's Stork Club by Willard Parker, this is the only recipe in the bar-book the Club published in 1946 to include tequila, emphasising its novelty value even at that late stage in human affairs. It was considered suitable as a morning refresher.

## CHIMAYO

**1½ measures silver tequila**

**1 measure strong still cider**

**¼ measure crème de cassis**

**¼ measure lemon juice**

Shake with ice, and strain into a cocktail glass. Garnish with a wedge of unpeeled red apple. Both this and the recipe below come from the *Cactus Cook Book* by Joyce L Tate, published by the Cactus and Succulent Society of America in 1971.

## JOSHUA PUNCH (for two)

**3 measures silver tequila**

**3 measures grapefruit juice**

**¼ measure lime juice**

**dash grenadine**

**1 prickly pear**

Peel and cube the prickly pear, and put in an electric blender with all the other ingredients and a handful of crushed ice. Blend for ten seconds on high speed, and strain into two chilled cocktail glasses. The recipe Mrs Tate was given, by the D'Arrigo Brothers Packing Company of Salinas, California, uses vodka rather than tequila, but the latter is much more in keeping with the spirit of the drink.

## FREDDY FUDPUCKER

**2 measures silver tequila**

**4 measures orange juice**

**½ measure Galliano**

Follow the same procedure as for the Harvey Wallbanger (see page 93), a variation of this drink.

## VIVA MARIA

**1 measure gold tequila**
**¼ measure maraschino**
**½ measure lime juice**
**dash grenadine**
**white of half an egg**

Shake well with ice, and strain into a champagne flute filled with crushed ice. Garnish with a twist of lemon and a cocktail cherry on a stick.

## MEXICAN WAVE

**1 measure gold tequila**
**¼ measure Galliano**
**¼ measure crème de banane**
**¼ measure double cream**
**dash grenadine**
**dash lemon juice**

Shake well with ice, and strain into a cocktail glass. Garnish with a half-slice of lemon. This drink, given in a cocktail book of 1979 by the late John Doxat, was originally called Sunrise, but we have taken the liberty of renaming it, to avoid confusion with the more familiar Tequila Sunrise (qv).

## TEQUADOR

**1 measure silver tequila**
**1½ measures pineapple juice**
**¼ measure lime juice**
**3 drops grenadine**

Shake the first three ingredients with ice, and strain into a champagne flute half-filled with crushed ice. Top the glass with more crushed ice, and then add three drops of grenadine, one after the other, into the centre of the drink, so that they sink in wisps of pale pink through the packed ice. Tequila cocktails with a dash of grenadine were very much the mood of the moment in the 1970s, and this one, given in Michael Walker's 1980 recipe book, is a typical performance drink.

## CORCOVADO

**1 measure silver tequila**

**1 measure blue curaçao**

**1 measure Drambuie**

**lemonade to top up**

Shake the first three ingredients with ice, and strain into a highball glass half-filled with cracked ice. Top with lemonade, and garnish with a half-slice of lemon. Drink through straws.

Here are a couple of contemporary updates of the classic Margarita:

## BLOODY MARGARITA

**1½ measures silver tequila**

**½ measure Cointreau**

**1 measure blood-orange juice (or Tropicana Sanguinello if you can't find the fresh fruit for squeezing)**

**½ measure lime juice**

Shake with ice, and strain into a chilled, unsalted cocktail glass.

## TANGERINE MARGARITA

**1½ measures añejo tequila**

**1 measure Cointreau**

**½ measure tangerine juice**

**½ measure lime juice**

Shake with ice, and strain into a chilled, salt-rimmed cocktail glass. This variant was invented by Fred McKibbon, bartender at the Grace Bar in New York.

## PEPPER EATER

**1 measure gold tequila**

**1 measure triple sec (or Cointreau)**

**1 tsp pieprzówka**

**1 measure orange juice**

**1 measure cranberry juice**

Shake with ice, and strain into a tumbler half-filled with cracked ice. Garnish with a whole red chilli pepper.

## FIREBIRD

**1½ measures silver tequila**

**½ measure crème de banane**

**½ measure lime juice**

**2 measures lemonade**

Add the ingredients in this order to a tumbler, half-filled with cracked ice. Garnish with a slice of lime.

## LAST CHANCE

**2 measures gold tequila**

**¼ measure apricot brandy**

**1 measure lime juice**

**1 tsp clear honey**

Shake well with ice and pour, without straining, into a tumbler. Garnish with a slice of lime.

## EXOTICA

**1½ measures gold tequila**

**¼ measure white crème de cacao**

**1 tsp Cointreau**

**1 measure mango juice**

**1 measure white grape juice**

**½ measure lime juice**

Shake with ice, and strain into a tumbler packed with cracked ice. Garnish extravagantly with tropical fruits.

## BUTTOCK CLENCHER

**1 measure silver tequila**

**1 measure gin**

**¼ measure Midori**

**2 measures pineapple juice**

**2 measures lemonade**

Shake the first four ingredients with ice, and strain into a tall narrow glass half-filled with cracked ice. Add the lemonade. Garnish with a pineapple chunk on a stick. This euphoniously named cocktail is given in Robert Cross's cocktail book of 1996.

## ROSARITA HIGHBALL

**2 measures silver tequila**
**½ measure crème de cassis**
**1 tsp lime juice**
**ginger ale to top up**

Shake the tequila, cassis and lime juice with ice, and strain into a tall glass half-filled with cracked ice. Top with ginger ale. Garnish with a slice of cucumber. This ingenious mixture was invented by New York and London bartender Dale Degroff.

## 209 EAST

**1 measure reposado tequila (strictly Sauza Hornitos)**
**¾ measure Cointreau**
**½ measure crème de fraise**
**¾ measure lime juice**

Shake with ice, and strain into a chilled cocktail glass. Another Dale Degroff creation, invented in 1995 for a couple of friends. Would that we all had friends like Dale.

And just in case the mood grabs you, here's how to slam. We strongly recommend that if a slamming session is to be convened, you consider covering the carpet and soft furnishings with waterproof sheeting.

## TEQUILA SLAMMER

**1 measure silver tequila**
**something chilled and sparkling (soda, lemonade, sparkling wine or champagne) to top up**

Pour the tequila into a shot glass, and top it up with the fizzy stuff. Covering the top of the glass with the palm of your hand, you strike it smartly against the bar counter or tabletop twice so it effervesces, uncover the glass and knock back the drink while it is still foaming.

# 8

# OTHER SPIRITS AND LIQUEURS

The cocktail scene would have been nothing, from the 1920s onwards anyway, without the liqueurs. One or two of the old traditional liqueurs, such as the monastic Chartreuse and Bénédictine, as well as the mid-nineteenth century orange inventions like Cointreau and Mandarine Napoléon, found their way into the mixed drinks of the turn of the twentieth century, but mostly they were drunk as they were, in tiny glasses fashioned expressly for the post-prandial purpose.

It was only with the cocktail boom of the twenties that the liqueurs started being treated with what can only be described as a little less reverence. This was the best thing that could have happened to them, in that it salvaged them from commercial obscurity, reinventing them as indispensable items of the cocktail cabinet.

The traditional aperitifs of France, absinthe and pastis, now found themselves being mixed with more than the customary slug of water, as they added aniseedy pungency – and, in absinthe's case, a weighty alcohol kick – to a cocktail.

To the curaçaos and brandy-based liqueurs, as well as the sweet, fruit-flavoured cordials, were gradually added a whole host of new products, together with some more venerable ones that were simply new to the export markets. Italy has always produced many old liqueurs, spirity potions infused with herbs and flowers, such as Strega and Galliano, and oddities like kümmel and goldwasser emerged from the shadows too to claim a piece of the action.

Not just these liqueurs, but a range of what are technically miscellaneous spirits, are included in the recipes in this chapter. These latter include Normandy's calvados, American applejack, Scandinavian akvavit, and kirsch. See the Glossary at the back of the book for definitions and descriptions of any of these products that may be unfamiliar to you.

Absinthe has enjoyed the most scandalous career of all the liqueurs. Banned in France in 1915 as a result of its association with the sordid deaths of the drink-dependent, it soon found itself *persona non grata* in other European countries too. It was wrongly thought that the wormwood it contains as a bitter flavouring was responsible in quantity for rotting the brain. In the 1990s, the drink was restored to us (although it remains illegal in France), much of it being made in the Czech Republic, where its strength ranges from a fairly austere 55% alcohol (the same as green Chartreuse, incidentally, which it has never been thought needful to ban) to a mighty 70%, although a Bulgarian product bottled at 85% suggests that the sky is indeed the limit for this product.

Whatever its strength, it is as well to heed the words of that repository of nineteenth-century alcohol knowledge, George Saintsbury, who declared of absinthe, 'Nobody but the kind of lunatic whom it was supposed to produce, and who may be thought to have been destined to lunacy, would drink it neat.' Indeed not. Its main serving ritual involved pouring it over a cube of sugar balanced on a perforated spoon, or, alternatively, soaking the sugar-cube in it and setting it alight before stirring it into the drink, but even in these preparations, it was sugared and watered. This procedure soon shaped up into its basic cocktail recipe.

## ABSINTHE COCKTAIL

**1 measure absinthe**

**1 measure still spring water**

**dash sugar syrup**

**dash Angostura bitters**

Shake with ice, and strain into a cocktail glass. Do not garnish.

## APPLE JACK

**1½ measures calvados**

**1½ measures sweet red vermouth**

**dash Angostura bitters**

Shake with ice, and strain into a cocktail glass. No garnish necessary. Despite its name, the preferred spirit for this cocktail was the French apple brandy, rather than its American cousin.

## ROSE

**1½ measures kirsch**

**1½ measures dry vermouth**

**1 tsp grenadine**

Shake with ice, and strain into a cocktail glass. Garnish with a cherry on a stick. This is one of three variants on a cocktail with this name, all involving kirsch, cherry brandy or both, given in the *Savoy Cocktail Book* (1930), but this is the (very dry) formula that seems to have stood the test of time.

And while we're at the bar of the Savoy:

## SAVOY HOTEL

**1 measure brown crème de cacao**

**1 measure Bénédictine**

**1 measure brandy**

Pour the ingredients, in this order, very carefully over the back of a spoon into a small, straight-sided glass, so that they stay in their separate layers. This cocktail introduces us to the world of the *pousse-café*, a novelty drink of the 1920s in which the ingredients are not mixed but sit one on top of the other. A few more will follow in this chapter. They may be worth trying once or twice to impress your friends (or perhaps your mother), but their appeal on the palate is somewhat limited, especially since the drink can never be iced, but must always be served at room temperature.

## SAVOY TANGO

**1½ measures applejack (or calvados)**

**1½ measures sloe gin**

Shake with ice, and strain into a cocktail glass. Garnish with a half-slice of lemon.

## APRICOT

**1½ measures apricot brandy**

**dash gin**

**¾ measure fresh orange juice**

**¾ measure lemon juice**

Shake with ice, and strain into a cocktail glass. Garnish with a thin slice of juicy-ripe apricot, unpeeled.

## THE MULE'S HIND LEG

**½ measure gin**
**½ measure Bénédictine**
**½ measure applejack**
**½ measure apricot brandy**
**½ measure maple syrup**

Shake with ice, and strain into a cocktail glass. Garnish with a twist of lemon peel. This is an enchantingly named, and very strong, cocktail from the 1920s. The pairing of apple brandy with apricot liqueur was a favoured combination of the twenties, as is demonstrated again below.

## ANGEL FACE

**1 measure calvados**
**1 measure apricot brandy**
**1 measure gin**

Shake with ice, and strain into a cocktail glass. Garnish with a half-slice of lemon. A lethally strong cocktail, not for beginners.

## MCCLELLAND

**2 measures sloe gin**
**1 measure white curaçao**
**dash absinthe**

Shake with ice, and strain into a cocktail glass. No garnish. We have not been able to discover the identity of the individual after whom this 1920s drink is named.

## PING-PONG

**1½ measures sloe gin**

**1½ measures crème d'Yvette (if not available, use Parfait Amour)**

**juice of a quarter of a lemon**

Shake with ice, and strain into a cocktail glass. Garnish with a twist of lemon.

## DEMPSEY

**1½ measures calvados**

**1½ measures gin**

**1 tsp absinthe**

**1 tsp grenadine**

Shake with ice, and strain into a cocktail glass. Named after the great champion boxer Jack Dempsey, this is guaranteed to land a killer blow.

## POOP DECK

**1½ measures crème de mûre**

**¾ measure ruby port**

**¾ measure brandy**

Shake with ice, and strain into a small wineglass. A sweet and fruity cocktail that should be drunk sparingly so that it doesn't cloy.

## YELLOW PARROT

**1 measure absinthe**

**1 measure yellow Chartreuse**

**1 measure apricot brandy**

Shake with ice, and strain into a cocktail glass filled with crushed ice, and garnished with a twist of lemon. This, and the cocktail below, indicate just what lengths of strength the drinker of the 1920s was prepared to go to in order to find the Holy Grail of a perfect mixed drink.

## XANTHIA

**1 measure gin**

**1 measure yellow Chartreuse**

**1 measure cherry brandy**

Shake with ice, strain into a cocktail glass filled with crushed ice, and garnish with a cherry on a stick.

## ALEXANDER'S SISTER

**1 measure gin**

**1 measure green crème de menthe**

**1 measure double cream**

Shake well with ice, and strain into a cocktail glass. The first experiments with cream cocktails in the twenties are not that appealing to us now, but there are a couple of exceptions. This and the original Brandy Alexander (qv) are two of them.

## OPAL

**2 measures absinthe**

**½ measure yellow Chartreuse**

**¼ measure still water**

Stir with ice in a mixing jug and pour, without straining, into a small wineglass. Add a half-slice of lemon.

## BLESSED EVENT

**2 measures applejack**

**2 measures Bénédictine**

**dash orange curaçao**

**juice of half a lime**

Shake with ice, and strain into a tumbler. Add a slice of lime.

## ADMIRAL

**1½ measures gin**

**1 measure cherry brandy**

**juice of half a lime**

Shake with ice, and strain into a cocktail glass. Decorate with a slice of lime and a cherry on a stick.

## POUSSE-CAFÉ

**½ measure grenadine**

**½ measure brown crème de cacao**

**½ measure maraschino**

**½ measure orange curaçao**

**½ measure crème d'Yvette (or Parfait Amour)**

**½ measure brandy**

Pour the ingredients very carefully in this order over the back of a spoon (using a clean spoon for each one) into a small, narrow glass, so that the layers remain separate. Whether or not this is the original pousse-café remains obscure, but it will be seen that the components of a layered cocktail are chosen primarily for their relative density, rather than their compatibility of flavour. As soon as you have put grenadine and chocolate liqueur into the same glass, you'll wish you hadn't. Anyway, if successful, the colour bands in this creation should go (reading downwards through the glass): amber, purple, orange, white, dark brown, red. Now, having congratulated yourself, you can throw it away, and make the next cocktail.

## TROPICAL COCKTAIL

**¾ measure brown crème de cacao**

**¾ measure maraschino**

**1¼ measures dry vermouth**

**dash orange bitters (or curaçao)**

Shake with ice, and strain into a small wineglass. Decorate with a twist of orange peel and a cherry.

## ALASKA

**2 measures gin**

**¾ measure yellow Chartreuse**

Stir with ice in a mixing jug, and strain into a tumbler on the rocks. We are almost finished with the yellow Chartreuse, we promise you, but this one is a fine and sophisticated cocktail from the early twentieth century that proved a long stayer in the cocktail repertoire, as long as people still wanted drinks that tasted of drink.

## DEVIL

**1½ measures brandy**

**1½ measures green crème de menthe**

Shake with ice, and strain into a cocktail glass. Garnish with a sprig of mint. We've already met the Little Devil (qv), and this is his big brother, effectively a green version of the Stinger (also qv).

## GOLDEN SLIPPER

**1 measure yellow Chartreuse**

**1 egg yolk**

**1 measure goldwasser**

Pour the Chartreuse into a tall sherry schooner. Drop the egg yolk on top of it without breaking it, and then add the glittery goldwasser. This won't in any way resemble a drink, either in taste or appearance, but we include it as a snapshot of the kind of activity with which New Yorkers tried to banish the wartime blues. It's from the *Stork Club Bar Book* (1946).

## WALLY

**1 measure applejack**

**1 measure peach brandy**

**1 measure lime juice**

Shake with ice, and strain into a cocktail glass. Add a slice of lime.

## LORRAINE

**1¾ measures kirsch**

**½ measure Bénédictine**

**juice of half a lime**

Shake with ice, and strain into a cocktail glass. Add a slice of lime and a cherry.

## SOUTHERN COMFORT COCKTAIL

**1¾ measures Southern Comfort**

**¾ measure Cointreau**

**juice of half a lime**

Shake with ice, and strain into a cocktail glass. Garnish with a slice of lime.

## AMERICAN FLAG

**½ measure grenadine**

**½ measure maraschino**

**½ measure crème d'Yvette (or Parfait Amour)**

Prepare as a pousse-café (see page 143), adding the ingredients carefully to a shot glass in this order. If nothing but a layered cocktail will do, this one isn't a bad mix of flavours. If you count the purple layer as blue, it comes out in the colours of Old Glory – and the Union Flag as well, for that matter.

## EAGLE

**1½ measures gin**

**¾ measure crème d'Yvette (or Parfait Amour)**

**juice of half a lemon**

**1 tsp caster sugar**

**white of an egg**

Shake very well with ice, to dissolve the sugar and amalgamate the egg white, and strain into a wineglass. Add a half-slice of lemon, and drink while still frothy.

## ROSALIND RUSSELL

**2 measures Danish akvavit**

**1 measure sweet red vermouth**

Stir with ice in a mixing jug, and strain into a small tumbler. Add a twist of lemon. This simple but adorable cocktail is another named after a movie star. Rosalind Russell was big news in the 1930s and 1940s, when she appeared in such films as *It Had To Happen* (1936) and *His Girl Friday* (1940).

## GLOOM CHASER

**1 measure Grand Marnier**

**1 measure orange curaçao**

**1 measure lemon juice**

**dash grenadine**

Shake with ice, and strain into a cocktail glass. Decorate with a twist of orange. A 1970s drink that should be seen as the antidote to the gin-based Gloom Raiser (qv).

## RHETT BUTLER

**1 measure Southern Comfort**

**1 measure orange curaçao**

**½ measure lemon juice**

**½ measure lime juice**

**soda water to top up**

Shake the first four ingredients with ice, and strain into a highball glass. Top with soda. Decorate with a half-slice of lemon and a slice of lime, and serve with straws. That liquor from the Southern States is what caused this cocktail to be named after the lead male character in Margaret Mitchell's Civil War novel *Gone With The Wind* (immortalised on screen in 1939 by Clark Gable).

## JADE

**1 measure golden rum**

**½ measure orange curaçao**

**½ measure green crème de menthe**

**½ measure lime juice**

Shake with ice, and strain into a cocktail glass. Add a slice of lime.

The cocktail boom of the 1970s and 1980s was very big on creamy concoctions, for which the liqueurs were quite indispensable. Here are a few.

## CARA SPOSA

**1 measure Tia Maria**

**1 measure orange curaçao**

**1 measure double cream**

Shake well with ice, and strain into a cocktail glass that has had its rim dipped in sugar. Very much an after-dinner drink.

## LEROY WASHINGTON

**1 measure brandy**

**½ measure Tia Maria**

**½ measure Drambuie**

**1 measure double cream**

Shake well with ice, and strain into a cocktail glass. Leave ungarnished.

## MANDARIN

**½ measure Galliano**

**½ measure Bénédictine**

**¾ measure apricot brandy**

**¾ measure Cointreau**

**1 tsp Mandarine Napoléon**

**1 measure orange juice**

**1 measure double cream**

Blend the ingredients with crushed ice in a liquidiser, and strain into a wineglass. Add a twist of orange peel.

## BANANA BLISS

**1 measure white rum**

**1 measure crème de banane**

**½ measure orange juice**

**dash Angostura bitters**

**dash grenadine**

**1 measure double cream**

Shake all but the grenadine well with ice, and strain into a tumbler. Sprinkle the grenadine in pink spots on the surface of the drink, and add a couple of slices of banana on a stick. This Michael Walker recipe, from his 1980 cocktail book, is simply fabulous.

## GRASSHOPPER

**1 measure green crème de menthe**

**1 measure white crème de cacao**

**1 measure double cream**

Shake well with ice, and strain into a cocktail glass. Sprinkle the surface with grated dark chocolate. This sweet, creamy cocktail could quite well take the place of a dessert. Its sensational chocolate-mint flavour has understandably made it a classic.

The contemporary era has discovered new spirits, such as South America's cachaça and pisco, and found new ways of incorporating liqueurs into some of the old classic preparations, such as the Martini.

## CAIPIRINHA

**2 measures cachaça**

**half a lime, cut into quarters**

**1 tsp sugar syrup**

Muddle the lime pieces and syrup in a mixing jug, pressing the lime pieces firmly to extract both the juice and oil from the skin. Now add the spirit and a few pieces of broken ice, and stir well. Decant the entire mixture, ice and all, into a rocks glass or tumbler. A beguilingly simple, and hugely popular, mixture that makes the most of its base ingredient, the sugar cane 'brandy' of South America. Use white rum instead of the cachaça for a Caipirissima, or good Russian vodka for a Caipiroska.

## PISCO SOUR

**2 measures pisco**

**half a lime**

**1 tsp sugar syrup**

**white of half an egg**

**dash Angostura bitters**

Squeeze the half of lime manually into a tumbler half-filled with cracked ice, and then drop the shell into the glass. Shake the pisco, sugar syrup and egg white well with more ice, and strain it into the prepared glass. Sprinkle a few drops of Angostura on top of the eggy froth. Some versions make do without the egg white, and even just mix the drink in the glass, but this seems to be the consensus version, and is more or less what Mr Walton was given when he drank his first Pisco Sour in Santiago, Chile, in 1992.

## ORANGE TREE

**¾ measure brandy**

**¾ measure Mandarine Napoléon**

**¾ measure apricot brandy**

**¾ measure mandarin juice (from a can of fruit)**

**2 measures lemonade**

Add all the ingredients to a tumbler half-filled with cracked ice, and stir gently. Garnish with a half-slice of orange.

## MELON BALL

**1 measure vodka**

**1 measure Midori**

**4 measures pineapple juice**

Shake with ice, and strain into a highball glass. Garnish with a ball of green-fleshed melon (Galia or Ogen) and a chunk of pineapple threaded on a cocktail stick.

## APOLLO 1

**1½ measures calvados**

**¾ measure Cointreau**

**½ measure Pimm's No 1**

Shake with ice, and strain into a rocks glass half-filled with cracked ice. Add a half-slice of orange.

## CAMEL'S COFFEE

**¾ measure Kahlua**

**½ measure brandy**

**½ measure white rum**

**½ measure Strega**

**1 measure lukewarm black coffee**

Shake with ice, and strain into a tumbler packed with ice-cubes. Add a couple of coffee beans.

## MOON RIVER

**1 measure gin**

**1 measure Cointreau**

**1 measure apricot brandy**

**½ measure Galliano**

**½ measure lime juice**

**½ measure sugar syrup**

**1 tsp blue curaçao**

Shake the first six ingredients with ice, and strain into a large wineglass with a little crushed ice in it. Sprinkle the blue curaçao across the surface of the drink.

## ALABAMA SLAMMER (serves six)

**1 measure Southern Comfort**

**1 measure vodka**

**1 measure sloe gin**

**4 measures fresh orange juice**

**2 tsp grenadine**

Shake the first four ingredients with ice, and strain into six shot glasses. Sprinkle a little grenadine on the surface of each. And then, in perfect coordination, all six of you should down the drink in one.

## MEXICAN MONK

**1 measure Kahlua**

**1 measure Frangelico**

**1 measure brown crème de cacao**

**½ measure sweet brown (oloroso) sherry**

**4 tbsp real vanilla ice-cream**

Blend the ingredients in a liquidiser, and strain into a tall glass. Grate a piece of dark chocolate into the drink. Cocktails with ice-cream in them became quite the thing in the 1990s. They taste like very grown-up milkshake. Below is another.

## BONAPARTE VELVET

**1 measure Napoleon brandy**

**1 measure Mandarine Napoléon**

**1 tsp Frangelico**

**3 tbsp real vanilla ice-cream**

Blend in the liquidiser, and strain into a tall glass. Garnish with a half-slice of orange.

## EVERGREEN

**1 measure crème de banane**

**½ measure gin**

**½ measure Midori**

**½ measure blue curaçao**

**2 measures white grape juice**

Shake with ice, and strain into a cocktail glass. Garnish with a seedless green grape on a stick.

## FORMULA 1

**2 measures vodka**

**¾ measure crème de fraise**

**¾ measure peach brandy**

**2 measures grapefruit juice**

**2 measures tonic water**

Add all the ingredients to a tall glass filled with cracked ice, and stir. Garnish with a twist of grapefruit peel and a small strawberry.

## SUMMER PASSION

**1 measure crème de fraise**

**1 measure passion-fruit juice**

**1 measure pineapple juice**

**1 measure lemonade**

Shake the first three ingredients with ice, and strain into a chilled wineglass. Add the lemonade, and garnish with a strawberry on a stick. A cocktail for a sizzling July afternoon outdoors. In contrast to:

## HELL FROZEN OVER

**1 measure sloe gin**

**1 measure dry vermouth**

**½ measure Mandarine Napoléon**

**½ measure apricot brandy**

Shake with ice, and strain into a cocktail glass. Add a cocktail cherry. One for a winter's night.

## GOLDEN SUNSET

**1½ measures Cointreau**

**1½ measures white crème de cacao**

**1½ measures double cream**

**¾ measure fresh orange juice**

**1 tsp Galliano**

Shake with ice, and strain into a large goblet-style wineglass. Add a twist of orange.

## EXTERMINATOR

**1 measure white rum**

**1 measure green Chartreuse**

Mix well in a tumbler filled with cracked ice. Add a half-slice of lemon. This drink, given in Robert Cross's cocktail book of 1996, will indeed finish you off.

And just in case veterans of the 1970s thought they had a monopoly on sexually suggestive cocktails, here is one that is blunt and to-the-point, and carries a visual innuendo too:

## BLOW JOB

**½ measure Grand Marnier**

**½ measure Kahlua**

**½ measure crème de banane**

**1 tsp pouring cream**

Shake the first three ingredients with ice, and strain into a shot glass. Float the cream on the surface of the drink. Swallow all at once.

# 9

# WINES, BEER AND CIDER

In this chapter, we turn finally to that category of drinks not immediately associated with cocktail-making, the fermented (and, in some cases, fortified) products of grape and grain.

Vermouth, of course, plays a very prominent role in the cocktail repertoire, as will have become apparent from the preceding chapters, and we include a few more recipes here in which it is indispensable, either in its dry or sweet versions. The other fortified wines – principal among them being port and sherry – were once used much more widely than they are now, as is hinted at by the fact that they each have their own particular methods of preparation by the cocktail bartender. There is a Port Wine Cocktail and a Sherry Cocktail, both to be found herein.

Many are the cocktails that use champagne. Indeed, 'top with champagne' became quite as nonchalant an instruction in cocktail recipes of the 1980s as 'top with soda' had once been. Be it noted that there is no sense in using the best stuff money can buy in these mixtures. You are not supposed to taste it for itself, but as part of a blend. Supermarket champagnes, and sparkling wines from other regions (especially if they are made by the same method as champagne) will do quite well enough.

Ordinary red and dry white table wines have only a limited range of applications, but we have thrown in a few recipes here for those who live in hope of finding something a little more stimulating to drink than a white wine spritzer (for which, however, we have also given the formula).

Beer and cider are the least used drinks of all in this context, outside the punches and hot drinks that were once a traditional feature of winter. Should these appeal, you will need to dig out that old punchbowl, or start scouring the car-boot sales if you haven't got one.

## WASSAIL BOWL (serves ten)

**3 litres good English, Scots or Welsh ale**
**20cl sweet brown sherry**
**10cl brandy**
**1 tsp ground nutmeg**
**1 tsp ground ginger**
**1 tsp ground cinnamon**
**125g soft brown sugar**
**10 apples, peeled, cored and baked until soft and fluffy**

Warm up all the ingredients except the apples in a very large saucepan until the sugar and spices are dissolved (no more than 10 minutes). Mash each apple while still warm, and divide them among six large mugs. Fill up each one with punch, and hand each guest a spoon for stirring the mushed-up apple into the drink. Alternatively, serve in cups, with a stick of cinnamon in each as a stirring implement. A bunch of frozen carol-singers coming to the end of the evening shift would be mighty glad of such a cheering cup.

A punch, hot or cold, was the traditional drink to be served at a large, festive gathering. They were generally lethally strong concoctions, served by being ladled out from a bowl into cups or glass mugs. The term derives from the Hindi word *panch*, meaning 'five', and denoting the basic five ingredients that originally went into them (these might be a spirit, a liqueur, fruit juice, some aromatic potion such as rosewater, and spices). During the nineteenth century, punches grew more elaborate and ostentatious, and were by no means always hot drinks, as is demonstrated by the following recipes included in Harry Craddock's Savoy book.

## CARDINAL PUNCH (generously serves two dozen)

**2 litres red wine (traditionally claret)**

**50cl brandy**

**50cl dark rum**

**50cl sparkling white wine**

**1 wineglass sweet red vermouth**

**2 litres sparkling water**

**500g caster sugar**

Mix together all but the sparkling wine and water in a large punchbowl with ice until all the sugar is dissolved. Add the fizzy ingredients at the last moment, and serve.

## CHAMPAGNE PUNCH (generously serves a dozen)

**3 bottles champagne**

**20cl brandy**

**20cl maraschino**

**20cl orange curaçao**

**75cl sparkling mineral water**

**250g caster sugar**

Add all the ingredients to a punchbowl with plenty of ice, and stir gently to dissolve the sugar. Garnish with seasonal fruits.

## BOMBAY PUNCH (serves dozens)

**1 litre sweet brown sherry**

**1 litre brandy**

**25cl orange curaçao**

**25cl maraschino**

**4 litres champagne or sparkling wine**

**2 litres sparkling water**

Add the ingredients to a punchbowl with a large quantity of cracked ice, and stir gently. Garnish with various sliced and chopped fruits in season. For smaller parties, the quantities in this hugely lavish punch can be scaled down proportionately.

A wine or cider cup, for serving at summer garden parties, was very like punch, but conceived on a more modest scale, and served from a jug instead of a bowl.

## RHINE WINE CUP (serves 8–10)

**1 litre sweet Rhine wine (go for a good Riesling, rather than the dreaded Liebfraumilch)**

**10cl maraschino**

**5cl orange curaçao**

**2 tsp caster sugar**

Mix the ingredients well with ice in a glass pitcher or claret jug, and decorate with slices of orange, pineapple and cucumber.

## CIDER CUP (serves 6–8)

**1 litre sweet cider**

**10cl maraschino**

**10cl orange curaçao**

**10cl brandy**

**50cl soda water**

Stir the first four ingredients with ice in a pitcher, and add the soda. Garnish with slices of apple and orange.

## CHAMPAGNE COCKTAIL

**¼ measure cognac**

**2 dashes Angostura bitters**

**1 sugar cube**

**well-chilled champagne to top up**

Drop the sugar cube into the bottom of a champagne flute, and add the Angostura. Agitate the sugar with a spoon to soak it in the bitters, before adding the brandy and then the champagne. Reportedly invented some time in the 1860s somewhere in the Southern States of America, the precise origins of this cocktail remain lost to record, but it has been an enduringly popular drink nonetheless, much taken still as a festive aperitif.

## KIR

**1 tsp crème de cassis**

**1 glass well-chilled dry white wine (traditionally Bourgogne Aligoté)**

Pour the wine over the liqueur, and stir. Aligoté is a speciality of the Burgundy region of France, a sharp-tasting, high-acid white wine. The practice of adding some of the traditional blackcurrant liqueur of Dijon arose as a way of sweetening its temper, but any not-too-fruity, acidic dry white can be used in its place. It is named in honour of a redoubtable mayor of Dijon, Félix Kir, a leader of the Resistance in Burgundy during the Second World War.

## KIR ROYALE

The high-roller's version of Kir is made by adding the liqueur to a glass of champagne, rather than still white wine. Ring the changes by adding crème de mûre (blackberry), crème de myrtille (bilberry) or crème de framboise (raspberry) instead of the cassis.

## PORT WINE COCKTAIL

**175ml good red port (LBV, or late-bottled vintage, quality is best)**

**2 dashes orange curaçao**

**1 dash orange bitters**

**1 dash Angostura bitters**

Stir with ice in a mixing jug, and strain into a wineglass. (In another version of the Port Wine Cocktail, the port is simply fired up with a dash of brandy, and has orange peel squeezed over the top.)

## SHERRY COCKTAIL

**175ml pale dry sherry (fino or manzanilla)**

**1 tsp dry vermouth**

**1 tsp orange bitters**

Stir with ice in a mixing jug, and strain into a wineglass. Garnish with a tiny bit of orange peel. This exceedingly dry cocktail makes an efficient aperitif.

## SHERRY TWIST (for two)

**3 measures pale dry sherry**

**1 measure brandy**

**1 measure dry vermouth**

**½ measure Cointreau**

**¼ measure lemon juice**

**pinch ground cinnamon**

Shake well with ice, and strain into two cocktail glasses. No garnish.

## SHERRY FLIP

**2 measures brown cream sherry**

**½ measure sugar syrup**

**1 egg, beaten**

Shake well with ice, and strain into a small wineglass. Sprinkle the surface with ground (or better still, freshly grated) nutmeg. Once thought suitable for the ladies, this preparation got rather forgotten when everybody started worrying about the wisdom of ingesting raw egg.

## SPRITZER

**3 measures chilled dry white wine**

**soda water to top up**

Add the ingredients in this order to a tall glass filled with broken ice, and garnish with a half-slice of lemon. The nearest thing to a temperance beverage the cocktail repertoire has, the spritzer became unaccountably popular in the 1980s, but now seems happily to be leaving us.

If you don't want to drink, don't drink. Or have a . . .

## SHANDY

Half-fill a tall glass with light lager, and top it up with lemonade. Once the only 'drink' that could legally be served outside the licensing hours in the UK.

## VERMOUTH-CASSIS

**125ml good French dry vermouth (e.g. Noilly Prat)**

**25ml crème de cassis**

**soda water to top up**

Add the ingredients in this order to a large wineglass, and give the drink a gentle stir. A very popular way of taking vermouth in the 1920s for those who found its dryness too uncompromising.

## NEGRONI

**1¼ measures sweet red vermouth**

**1 measure gin**

**¾ measure Campari**

Stir with ice in a mixing jug, and strain into a small tumbler. Decorate with a half-slice of orange and a cocktail cherry. This incomparably clever cocktail was invented unwittingly by a customer called Mr Negroni at a bar in Florence just after the First World War. It is one of the very best aperitif cocktails of all. Some add a dash of soda, but it does quite well enough without.

## FRENCH 75

**2 measures gin**

**1 tsp caster sugar**

**juice of half a lemon**

**champagne to top up**

Shake the first three ingredients well with ice to dissolve the sugar, and strain into a tall champagne flute. Top with champagne. American troops serving in France in the Great War took this cocktail back home with them at the conclusion of hostilities. It will be seen that it is basically a rather luxurious Gin Fizz.

## BLACK VELVET

Half-fill a straight-sided beer glass with cold Guinness, and then top it up with well-chilled champagne. This was invented at Brooks' Club in London in 1861, in honour of the recently departed Prince Albert.

## BELLINI

**1½ measures peach juice**

**chilled champagne to top up**

Add to a tall champagne flute in this order. Stir briefly and very gently. The Bellini was invented in the 1940s at Harry's Bar in Venice, where it is still the house cocktail, on the occasion of an exhibition in the city of works by the old master Giovanni Bellini.

## GLORIA SWANSON'S COCKTAIL

**2 measures fine cognac**

**chilled champagne to top up**

Add to a highball glass with a couple of cubes of ice in it. Decorate with a twist of lemon. Miss Swanson was possibly the most flamboyant of the early Hollywood aristocracy, and reputedly liked nothing better than to start the day with one of these.

## VERY MERRY WIDOW

**1½ measures gin**

**1½ measures red Dubonnet**

Stir with ice in a mixing jug, and strain into a cocktail glass. Add a twist of lemon. Dubonnet is one of that class of aromatised fortified wines that rises above everyday vermouth in its bitter, quinine-scented complexity.

Cocktails involving vermouth and dry sherry were a common feature of early twentieth-century bar lists. They were nearly always stirred rather than shaken, so as not to upset the sherry too much. Here are a few.

## CORONATION

**1½ measures pale dry sherry**
**1½ measures dry vermouth**
**dash maraschino**
**2 dashes orange bitters (or curaçao)**

Stir with ice in a mixing jug, and strain into a cocktail glass. Another very dry aperitif cocktail, created on the occasion of the coronation of George V in 1911.

## MR NEW YORKER

**1¾ measures dry vermouth**
**½ measure pale dry sherry**
**½ measure gin**
**dash Cointreau**

Stir with ice in a mixing jug, and strain into a cocktail glass.

## ARMOUR

**1¾ measures pale dry sherry**
**1 measure sweet red vermouth**

Stir with ice in a mixing jug, and strain into a cocktail glass. Add a twist of lemon.

## BAMBOO

**2 measures pale dry sherry**

**¾ measure sweet red vermouth**

Stir with ice in a mixing jug, and strain into a cocktail glass. This is the slightly drier version of the above, and the one that became a classic formula for as long as such combinations were in vogue.

## VICTORY

**1 measure dry vermouth**

**1 measure sweet red vermouth**

**¼ measure fresh orange juice**

**¼ measure lemon juice**

**2 dashes grenadine**

Shake with ice, and strain into a cocktail glass. Add twists of orange and lemon.

## OPERATOR

**2 measures chilled dry white wine**

**2 measures ginger ale**

**1 tsp lime juice**

Add the ingredients to a tumbler containing a couple of pieces of ice, and garnish with a slice of lime. A wine-based version of the Moscow Mule, for those who find vodka a bit too much to take.

When package holidays to the Costa del Sol took off in the economically dynamic 1960s, British holidaymakers brought home the taste for a Spanish drink that had refreshed them on the beaches, and it wasn't dry sherry.

## SANGRIA (serves 6–8)

**1 bottle Spanish red wine (ordinary non-Reserva Rioja will do)**
**4 measures Spanish brandy**
**juice of an orange**
**juice of a lime**
**1 tbsp caster sugar**

Add all the ingredients to a large glass pitcher with plenty of cracked ice, and stir to dissolve the sugar. It should be served in tall glasses with slices of citrus fruit floating in it. Some pep it up by splashing a little soda water or lemonade into each serving, but it came to be preferred as a strictly still drink.

## CARIBBEAN CHAMPAGNE

**¼ measure golden rum**
**¼ measure crème de banane**
**dash Angostura bitters**
**chilled champagne to top up**

Add the ingredients in this order to a champagne flute. Stir gently, and garnish with a thin slice of banana on a cocktail stick. Another drink to evoke memories of sun-kissed 1970s package holidays.

## HONEYDEW

**50g chopped honeydew melon**
**1 measure gin**
**dash Pernod**
**½ measure lemon juice**
**chilled champagne to top up**

Blend the first four ingredients with crushed ice in a liquidiser, and strain into a large wineglass. Top with champagne, and garnish with a ball of melon on a cocktail stick.

## BUCK'S FIZZ

**2 measures orange juice (pressed juice from a carton, not freshly squeezed)**
**chilled champagne to top up**

Add the ingredients in this order to a champagne flute or wineglass. Although it became very popular in the 1980s, Buck's Fizz had been invented as long ago as 1921. Once the height of sophistication, it gradually became a useful way to disguise thin, acidic champagne. It is actually better made with a quality sparkling wine from California or Australia.

## RESTORATION

**2 measures red wine**
**½ measure brandy**
**½ measure crème de framboise**
**dash lemon juice**
**soda water to top up**

Add the ingredients in this order to a highball glass half-filled with cracked ice. Stir gently, and garnish with a couple of raspberries on a cocktail stick.

## INIGO JONES

**1 measure rosé wine (try Argentinian)**

**1 measure marsala dolce**

**1 measure brandy**

**dash lemon juice**

**dash fresh orange juice**

Stir with ice in a mixing jug, and strain into a tumbler half-filled with cracked ice. Add a half-slice of orange. One of the very rare cocktails to contain pink wine.

## TROPICAL PORT

**2 measures red port (LBV quality)**

**1 measure pineapple juice**

**1 measure orange juice**

**dash lemon juice**

**1 measure soda water**

Combine the ingredients in a large wineglass filled with cracked ice, and garnish with a half-slice of lemon and a couple of pineapple chunks.

## BURLINGTON

**2 measures red wine**

**1 sweet red vermouth**

**1 measure calvados**

**soda water to top up**

Stir the first three ingredients with ice in a mixing jug, and pour without straining into a highball glass. Top with soda. Add a twist of orange peel, and serve with straws.

## BIRETTA

**3 measures medium-dry white wine (such as Vouvray demi-sec)**

**1 measure dry vermouth**

**½ measure gin**

**½ measure orange curaçao**

**2 dashes Angostura bitters**

Stir with ice in a mixing jug, and strain into a large wineglass. Garnish with a half-slice of orange.

## PORT IN A STORM

**2 measures red wine**

**1½ measures port**

**½ measure brandy**

Stir with ice in a mixing jug, and strain into a wineglass half-filled with cracked ice.

## ROMAN HOLIDAY

**½ measure gin**

**½ measure sweet red vermouth**

**dash lemon juice**

**chilled dry white wine to top up (Italian for preference, such as Frascati Superiore)**

Shake the first three ingredients with ice, and strain into a tumbler. Top with white wine. Then you can imagine you are either Gregory Peck or Audrey Hepburn in the film of the same name, as the case may be.

## RED PASSION

**2 measures full-bodied red wine** (**e.g. Australian Shiraz**)

**½ measure passion-fuit syrup**

**2 measures ginger ale**

Add the ingredients in this order to a wineglass that has been frosted in the freezer.

## CANTON

**1½ measures shao-shing**

**¼ measure Cointreau**

**2 measures mandarin juice** (**from a can of unsweetened fruit**)

**1 tsp grenadine**

Shake with ice, and strain into a tumbler half-filled with cracked ice. Add a twist of orange. If you can't find the Chinese version of rice wine, use Japanese sake, but then you may have to rename the drink accordingly.

## FANTAISIE

**well-chilled medium-dry white wine** (**e.g. Vouvray sec, or German Riesling Spätlese**)

**¾ measure apricot brandy**

Add the liqueur to a small frosted glass of medium white wine. A sweeter variation on the Kir principle.

## CRIMEAN

**2 measures dry white wine**

**¾ measure Cointreau**

**grated zest of a lemon**

**1 measure soda water**

Stir the first three ingredients with ice in a mixing jug, and pass through a tea-strainer (to filter out the zest) into a cocktail glass. Add the soda, and garnish with a twist of lemon.

## MAGGIE MAY

**3 measures sparkling red Lambrusco**

**1 measure dry vermouth**

**¾ measure crème de framboise**

Add the ingredients in this order to a frosted champagne flute, and decorate with a raspberry on a cocktail stick. Believe us, this is a much more appealing proposition than drinking the sparkling red Lambrusco on its own.

## SOUTHERN TANGO

**1 measure dry vermouth**

**½ measure Southern Comfort**

**2 measures lemonade**

Add the ingredients in this order to a tumbler half-filled with cracked ice. Add a half-slice of lemon.

## LONDON FIZZ

**3 measures chilled champagne**

**1 measure mandarin juice**

**1 measure grapefruit juice**

**1 tsp passion-fruit syrup**

Add the ingredients in this order to a frosted champagne flute, and dangle a twist of grapefruit peel in the glass.

## CORNUCOPIA

**3 measures champagne**

**¼ measure Grand Marnier**

**¼ measure Campari**

**¼ measure grenadine**

Add the ingredients in this order to a frosted champagne flute. Add a twist of orange peel.

## GAGARIN

**1 measure vodka**

**½ measure crème de cassis**

**½ measure cherry brandy**

**1 tsp lime juice**

**champagne to top up**

Stir the first four ingredients with ice in a mixing jug, and strain into a champagne flute. Top with champagne. Created by Austrian bartender Fritz Schaller for the Bols liqueur corporation, to honour the world's first cosmonaut, Yuri Gagarin. The original recipe used the sparkling perry Babycham, now enjoying a modest come-back, for topping up.

## GOOD LUCK

**1 measure white rum**

**½ measure strained sweetened raspberry purée**

**champagne to top up**

Mix the purée into the rum in a frosted champagne flute. Top with champagne. Stir gently once more. Garnish with a raspberry on a cocktail stick.

## CHAMPAGNE CRANBERRY PUNCH (comfortably makes around 24 servings)

**1 bottle champagne**

**25cl crème de cassis**

**5cl lime juice**

**4 tbsp clear honey**

**1 litre cranberry juice**

**50cl sparkling mineral water**

Dissolve the honey in the cranberry juice with ice in a punchbowl, and then mix in all the other ingredients. Garnish with slices of lime. A modern-day punch for a summer party. It is reasonably innocuous. As a contrast, you might go for the . . .

## KNOCKOUT PUNCH (around 10 servings)

**1 litre sweet cider**

**1 measure gin**

**1 measure Bénédictine**

**1 measure brandy**

**1 measure peach brandy**

**25cl lemonade**

Add the ingredients to a large pitcher with plenty of ice.

## SOMERSET PUNCH (12–14 servings)

**1 litre strong dry Somerset cider**

**15cl dry white wine**

**2 measures calvados**

**15cl orange juice**

**15cl apple juice**

**1 measure lemon juice**

**30cl ginger ale**

Mix the ingredients in a punchbowl with plenty of ice. Add slices of apple and orange.

# 10

# THE MORNING AFTER

What a swell party it was! Except that you have woken up this morning feeling as though you had perhaps expired in your sleep, and have since been cast into the fiery furnace where you undoubtedly belong.

Some lucky souls never suffer from alcohol hangovers, which generally means not that they couldn't get one, merely that they have learned what their systems will take, in what proportions and combinations. This is known scientifically as 'The Sensible Approach'. And while we may devoutly wish each hangover to be the last, the likelihood is it won't be. What, as the great revolutionist Mr Lenin once inquired, is to be done?

'Don't drink!' one's doctor may cry, but if you have bought our little book, we may presume that this is not likely to be a short- or medium-term option. On the time-honoured principle that prevention is better than cure, though, there are recourses one can take to evade any possible negative after-effects the next day.

Drink a half-pint of whole milk before embarking on a session. The lactic fat lines the stomach, and helps to protect it against the corrosive impact of spirituous drinks.

Drink a large glass of water between the alcoholic drinks. If it seems a tedious business, tell yourself you are merely cleansing your palate between cocktails.

Drink a pint of water at the end of it all, before collapsing into bed. The worst of a hangover's effects are caused by dehydration of the system, so let it know that you haven't forgotten it.

Eat. Even if it is purely a cocktail soirée rather than a dinner party that is being planned, have plenty of nibbles on hand. Savoury snacks of one sort or another (olives, nuts, cheese, twiddles of cured meats and smoked salmon, sandwich-filler loaded on to celery sticks, and suchlike) will do well, but try to avoid a preponderance of salty items, which will only exacerbate the all-round raising of blood pressure involved in prolonged alcohol intake.

If it should be that these precautions have failed (or been forgotten), then the hangover must be stoically endured. There are really only two cures now, one being immediate resort to a proprietary painkiller, and the other the passage of time. Whatever painkiller you choose always first check the advice both on and inside the packet. One gram of aspirin gets to work quickly enough, but doctors advise anyone with asthma not to take it and aspirin should also be avoided if you have a sensitive stomach (turbulent nausea is quite as likely a hangover symptom as the pounding head). Paracetamol is just as good as an alternative less likely to cause trouble for asthmatics, though you should check with your doctor if you have any concern; however it is not recommended for those with delicate livers (in which case, you shouldn't have been boozing to excess either). Ibuprofen (again, not to be used by asthmatics), being principally an anti-inflammatory painkiller, is, in our experience, less effective against a severe headache.

Other ways of counteracting that overall ill-at-ease feeling that threatens to last all morning are many and various. Some like nothing better than a hearty fried breakfast, insisting that an intake of fats helps to mitigate the biliousness. For others, it could only augment it. More whole milk, if you can square up to it, is quite soothing, as it helps to neutralise the excess acids in the stomach. Still others believe in distracting the body and mind with some other theme, such as engaging in the sexual act, or at least imagining it, or choosing now as the morning to do something you have been putting off for too long, such as tidying up the garage or starting *Anna Karenina*.

A cup of hot water with the juice of half a lemon squeezed into it is a constructive thing to take. As long as it is swallowed before any other food or drink in the morning, the lemon acts to flush the liver of accumulated toxins.

There is also the hair-of-the-dog option, the idea that a little more alcohol will at least grant you a stay of execution. This can partially, imperfectly work, however reckless or repulsive it may seem. A spicy, nutritious Bloody Mary (qv) is one of the world's best hangover drinks, because it is full of aggressive flavours and yet you can't taste the alcohol in it. If the thought of even that discreet slug of vodka is too much, have it without, in which case, you should technically refer to the drink as a Virgin Mary, although you will probably not just at the minute give a tinker's cuss for what the damn thing is called, as long as it does the job required of it.

Other tried-and-true, or at least tried-and-traditional, mixtures are:

## PRAIRIE OYSTER

**1 measure good cognac**
**dash malt vinegar**
**yolk of an egg, unbroken**
**½ tsp Worcestershire sauce**
**3 dashes Tabasco**

Add the ingredients to a small tumbler in this order. Do not stir the drink, but down it in one with the head tilted right back and the tongue flat, so that the egg yolk slides over the tongue and only breaks in the throat. (In other words, it is swallowed like the oyster in the drink's name.) It is as well to have some sparkling water or something similar on hand, to counteract the appalling taste and texture of this drink.

## SAVOY CORPSE REVIVER

**1 measure brandy**

**1 measure white crème de menthe**

**1 measure Fernet Branca**

Shake with ice until very cold, and strain into a cocktail glass. Fernet Branca is a bitter tonic spirit from Italy, especially recommended for the morning after. Added to a Stinger, as here, it might just do the trick, and will leave the mouth feeling minty-fresh, as though you had just brushed your teeth on a perfectly normal morning.

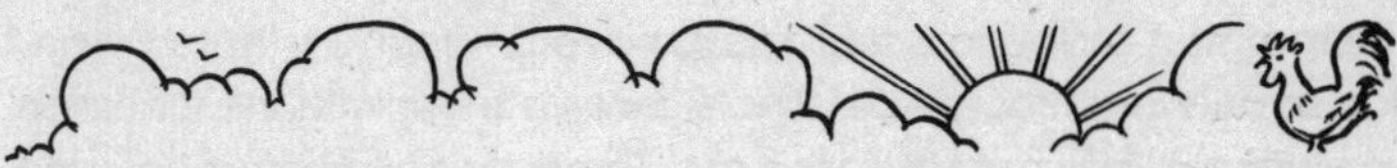

## MORNING FIZZ

**1 measure bourbon**

**¼ measure Pernod**

**white of half an egg**

**½ tsp caster sugar**

**dash lemon juice**

**soda water to top up**

Shake with ice, and strain into a tall glass. Top with soda.

If the thought of more alcohol doesn't appeal (and there is no reason that it should), try an enlivening non-alcoholic cocktail, but try to avoid orange juice, as it can irritate the stomach more than other fruit juices.

## GODCHILD

**1 measure blackcurrant cordial**

**dash lemon juice**

**lemonade to top up**

Fill a tall glass with ice-cubes, add the ingredients in this order, and stir to mix.

## PIPPIN

**3 measures apple juice (pressed style, not concentrate)**
**dash lemon juice**
**dash grenadine**
**ginger ale to top up**

Fill a tall glass with ice-cubes, add the ingredients in this order, and stir to mix. Drink through straws if it makes you feel better.

A final note: milk thistle, a herbal remedy that we have found helpful is available in capsule form from health-food stores. Research tells us that it can assist in the regeneration of liver cells. The product makes a useful dietary supplement for those whose line of duty (or hedonistic instincts) involve them with the ingestion of alcoholic liquor on a daily basis. The signs of a liver performing at less than full function include a tendency to perspire at the slightest effort, a haunting ache in the upper part of the right shoulder, and a tender feeling – perhaps accompanied by a rumbling like that of an empty stomach – on the right side of the upper chest. Best have a medical check-up if you have these symptoms, but also put yourself on a modest dose of milk thistle, taken with food. As with all such products, follow the advice that comes with your supply.

# GLOSSARY

A listing of some of the less familiar products used throughout this book (together with their typical alcohol strengths, expressed as a percentage by volume).

**Absinthe** Toweringly strong green aperitif liqueur, flavoured with aniseed and wormwood, nowadays a speciality product of eastern Europe. (55–70%)

**Akvavit** Grain- or potato-based Scandinavian spirit aromatised with spices. (40% or more)

**Amaretto** Very sweet, amber-coloured Italian liqueur flavoured with almonds, and tasting strongly of marzipan. (28%)

**Angostura bitters** Rum-based bitter infused with gentian root and herbs, of South American origin, now made in Trinidad. Added in dashes to season a cocktail. (45%)

**Applejack** American brandy distilled from apples, similar in style to France's calvados. (40%)

**Apricot brandy** Amber-coloured liqueur flavoured with apricots, sometimes known as abricotine. France's Lejay-Lagoute is the best brand. (20–28%)

**Bailey's Irish Cream** A smooth Dublin blend of whiskey, cocoa and cream. (17%)

**Bénédictine** Amber-coloured, originally monastic liqueur from Normandy, flavoured with honey, herbs and spices. (40%)

**Cachaça** Brazilian sugar cane spirit distilled from fermented cane juice rather than molasses, as with rum. (39–40%)

**Calvados** An amber-coloured brandy distilled from apples in the Normandy region of northern France. (40%)

**Campari** Vivid red Italian bitter aperitif flavoured with herbs, spices and orange peel. (25%)

**Chartreuse** Monastic liqueur still made by Carthusian monks from a blend of over 100 wild and cultivated herbs. Comes in two colours, a syrupy, minty yellow and a more pungently herbaceous green. (Yellow 40%, green 55%)

**Cherry brandy** Deep red liqueur flavoured with cherries (most often the black varieties). (24–28%)

**Cointreau** Colourless, sweet, French orange-flavoured liqueur invented in the mid-nineteenth century. (40%)

**Crème d'Yvette** Aromatic liqueur flavoured with violets. (40%)

**Crème de banane** Bright yellow liqueur flavoured with bananas. (24–30%)

**Crème de cacao** Chocolate-flavoured liqueur in two colours, sweet dark brown and even sweeter white. (Brown around 25%, white around 20%)

**Crème de cassis** Deep purple liqueur flavoured with black-currants, a speciality of the Burgundy region. (20%)

**Crème de fraise** Bright red liqueur flavoured with strawberries. (25%)

**Crème de framboise** Bright red liqueur flavoured with raspberries. (25%)

**Crème de menthe** Peppermint-flavoured liqueurs in two colours, sweet bright green and less piercingly flavoured white. (24–25%)

**Crème de mûre** Deep purple liqueur flavoured with blackberries. (25%)

**Crème de myrtille** Deep purple liqueur flavoured with bilberries (blueberries). (25%)

**Crème de noyau** Almondy-flavoured, slightly pinkish liqueur made from the stones of peaches and apricots. (Around 30%)

**Curaçao** Generic name for a range of originally Caribbean liqueurs made by steeping bitter oranges in a neutral base spirit. Can be colourless (known as triple sec), orange, blue, green, red or yellow. (25–30%)

**Drambuie** Scotch-based liqueur flavoured with heather honey and herbs, once made on the Isle of Skye. (40%)

**Fernet Branca** Medicinal Italian bitter sold as a tonic for hang-overs. (40%)

**Frangelico** Pale straw-coloured, sweet Italian liqueur flavoured with hazelnuts and herbs. (24%)

**Galliano** Bright yellow Italian liqueur flavoured with vanilla, star-anise and many other herbs and spices. (35%)

**Genever** Traditional Dutch version of gin. (40%)

**Goldwasser** Clear, sweet liqueur flavoured with aniseed and caraway, and speckled with particles of real gold. Once a speciality of Danzig (Gdansk). (40%)

**Grand Marnier** Sweet, amber-coloured French orange liqueur made by steeping bitter oranges in cognac, and cask-ageing it. (40%)

**Grenadine** Non-alcoholic, or very slightly alcoholic, sweet red syrup flavoured with pomegranate. (0–3%)

**Kahlua** Deep brown, sweet Mexican coffee liqueur with a hint of bitterness. (26.5%)

**Kirsch** Colourless distillate of cherries produced across northern Europe. (40%)

**Kümmel** Clear, sweet, traditionally Latvian liqueur flavoured with caraway seeds. (38–39%)

**Limonnaya** Traditional style of vodka flavoured with lemon. (40%)

**Mandarine Napoléon** Amber-coloured, sweet Franco-Belgian liqueur flavoured with tangerines. (38%)

**Maraschino** Colourless Italian liqueur flavoured with the Marasca red cherry variety. (32–50%)

**Marsala Dolce** Sweetest version of the brown fortified wine of Sicily. (17–18%)

**Metaxa** Grape brandy from Greece, tasting sweet and toffeeish compared to cognac. (40%)

**Midori** Bright green, very sweet Japanese melon liqueur. (20%)

**Parfait Amour** Violet-coloured, violet- and vanilla-flavoured, citrus-based sweet liqueur. (Around 30%)

**Passoa** Passion-fruit liqueur made by the Cointreau group. (20%)

**Peach brandy** Amber-coloured liqueur flavoured with peaches. (20–28%)

**Pernod** Pale yellow pastis (aniseed liqueur) made in northern France. (40%)

**Pieprzówka** Traditional style of vodka flavoured with hot peppers. (45%)

**Pimm's No 1 Cup** Proprietary English bitter-sweet cordial intended for blending with lemonade or soda as a summer drink. (25%)

**Pisco** Colourless Peruvian or Chilean spirit made from Muscat grapes. (35–43%)

**Shao-shing** The fermented rice wine of China. (17–18%)

**Sloe gin** Gin infused with sloes, the fruit of the blackthorn shrub. A traditional English preparation. (26%)

**Southern Comfort** Whiskey-based liqueur from the southern states of the USA, flavoured, among other things, with peaches. (40%)

**Strega** Bright yellow, sweet herbal liqueur from Italy. (40%)

**Swedish Punch** (Svensk Punsch) Rum-based, cask-aged liqueur, with additions of wine, herbs and spices such as cinnamon and cloves. (26%)

**Tia Maria** Deep brown, syrupy Jamaican coffee liqueur. (26.5%)

**Van der Hum** Generic name for South African sweet orange liqueurs, based on Cape brandy infused with *naartjes*, an indigenous small orange variety. (25% or more)

# INDEX

*Cocktail names are shown in bold.*